The People of Gower

The People of Gower

by

Derek Draisey

Draisey Publishing

DRAISEY PUBLISHING
77 Geiriol Road
Townhill,
Swansea, SA1 6QR

First published in 2003 by Draisey Publishing
Reprinted 2004
Copyright © Derek Draisey 2003

ISBN 0 9546544 0 4

Set in Times and Garamond by Logaston Press
and printed in Great Britain by
Bell and Bain, Glasgow

Contents

Acknowledgements

To Ann for all her love and patience, for all her help and support, and for her proof reading. Special thanks to the staff at Swansea Library for their commendable assistance and their advice on matters pertaining to research; in particular to Mrs M. Jones for her unstinting kindness.

The majority of the photographs, maps and illustrations in this book are my own work, but I would like to specifically thank the clergy and the Church in Wales for permitting me to photograph Gower churches, tombstones and effigies; and the Royal Commission on Ancient and Historical Monuments in Wales for permission to publish a plan of the Roman fort at Loughor.

Preface

'History', someone rightly said, 'is people'. Without people there would be no megalithic tombs, no artefacts waiting to be found, no record of the events of long ago. In Gower, as elsewhere, there was no one people, rather a succession of different people, each with a distinctive culture, a contrastive language. Even when cultures merged after long periods of coexistence the people of Gower were still subject to change, for they did not live in isolation, but were affected by outside influences and by significant events that had taken place elsewhere. The object of this work is, therefore, threefold—to provide a summary of the various cultures that have taken root in Gower from Stone Age times to the period of Anglo-Norman domination; to trace the origins of these cultures and show how they have left their mark on the local landscape and in ancient manuscripts relating to Gower; to present some of the material in the wider context of Wales and Britain, with the emphasis, in Chapters Three, Four and Five on the evolutionary development of the *Cymry* and their loss of independence to the Anglo-Normans.

CHAPTER I
Prehistoric Man

What is Gower? A peninsula which the sea has formed by battering the cliffs on its southern coast and flooding the Llanrhidian Sands to the north? It is more than that, surely. In times past Gower has experienced ice ages in which snow, accumulating on high ground, became moving sheets of ice (glaciers), stripping away soil and rock as they ground their way down through the valleys, at the same time spreading over hills and lowlands to halt (on one occasion) as far south as Cefn Bryn. Whenever the temperature rose the ice retreated and the climate improved, at times becoming so warm that Gower became home to exotic animals such as the straight-tusked elephant, the soft-nosed rhinoceros and the hippopotamus.

So how did the remnants of such large animals come to be deposited in Gower caves? The answer, of course, is that portions of these herbivores were taken there by carnivores. In colder times, certainly, Gower caves have served as dens for cave bears, cave lions, cave hyenas and wolves. The hyenas seem out of place in a cold climate, but their bones have been found in several Gower caves. One can imagine them snapping and snarling over a carcass, the cave floors littered with bones, the stench of raw flesh and excrement filling the dark interiors—but there was yet another predator to compete for shelter in the Gower caves.

Neanderthal Man

The remains of a Neanderthal man have been found in North Wales, and the bones of these early humans suggest that they were ugly by our standards, with retreating foreheads and massive brow-ridges, almost like apes. They were also robust, their short limbs making them well suited to living in a cold environment, their extremities being closer to the heart. No such remains have been found in Gower, but Neanderthal man certainly roamed the plateau above the present coastline. It is known, for example, that a stone handaxe found at Rhosili had been fashioned by a Neanderthal about 100,000 years ago. The question, then, is how do we know the handaxe belonged to these early men?

The technological advances of Prehistoric man are classified according to the materials he used—stone, bronze or iron. The term Palaeolithic means Old Stone Age, and Palaeolithic man is believed to have first set foot in Wales about 250,000 years ago.

In archaeological terms the Lower and Middle Palaeolithic periods relate to lower levels in the stratigraphy in which we would expect to find the oldest artefacts, and it has long been established by association that the oldest artefacts in Europe are the work of Neanderthal man.

He certainly knew how to knap flint; that is, to strike it in such a way as to sheer off fragments that had a sharp edge, ideal for cutting raw flesh and scraping skins. The kind of stone he preferred to use was flint, but this can only be obtained in Wales from beaches, usually in the form of small pebbles. There was, however, a similar material called chert, found in the local limestone, which, although coarser grained, was just as effective. A distinctive chert flake found in one cave has been classified as Mousterian, meaning that it belonged to a late phase in Neanderthal technology, roughly 70-30,000 B.C., although there are many who would question the classification of this particular flake.

Homo sapiens

By 30,000 B.C. Neanderthal man appears to have become extinct, leaving no tangible clues as to why this should be. His disappearance may have had something to do with the arrival in Europe, about 36,000 B.C., of *Homo sapiens*—modern man, long-limbed and, therefore, taller than their short-limbed neighbours. *Homo sapiens'* technology in stone was more advanced and, being younger than Neanderthal man's Mousterian technology, its position in the stratigraphy is referred to as the Upper Palaeolithic.

When *Homo sapiens* came to Gower they did so at a time when Britain was joined to the European mainland, the sea level being much lower than it is today. The climate would have been colder then, and Gower stood out as a plateau, overlooking the vast grassland (tundra) that has subsequently been flooded by the Britsol Channel. From caves situated in the southern slopes of the Gower plateau, *Homo sapiens* observed the huge herds of grazing animals that roamed the tundra—herds of mammoth, reindeer and bison. The bones, teeth, tusks and horns of these and other animals have been found in a number of Gower caves, the most notable being Goat's Hole, otherwise known as Paviland, where the cold fauna has been catalogued as follows:

Carnivores: cave hyena and cave lion (both rare), wolf (uncommon) and cave bear (quite common, perhaps because man killed it for its skin)

Herbivores: mammoth (rare), Irish elk (uncommon); particularly numerous were the remains of wild horse which appears to have been targeted by early Homo sapiens all over Europe; also woolly rhinoceros, wild ox and especially reindeer, for another cave yielded over 1000 antlers.

Other caves have yielded the remains of arctic hare, arctic fox, arctic lemming, European bison and red deer.

Paviland is the richest cave in Britain when it comes to Palaeolithic tools—more than 5,000 artefacts have been catalogued to date, but back in 1913 a Frenchman examined about 3,600 flakes and fragments and declared that at least 800 were tools. Stone tools are grouped into industries according to the way they were fashioned, and the majority of tools found at Paviland belong to the Aurignacian industry, the work of *Homo sapiens*. It is possible that all the Gower caves were occupied by *Homo sapiens*, but only Paviland, Long Hole and North Hill Tor Cave have yielded artefacts that can be confidently classified as Aurignacian. Like the Mousterian industry of Neanderthal man, the Aurignacian industry provided tools for the big game hunters, spearheads and the like.

The Red Lady of Paviland

The period 26-8,000 B.C. is one in which there is little evidence for human settlement in Britain due, no doubt, to the Late Devensian Ice Age. Yet Paviland has provided evidence of occupation at an early stage in this particular ice age. In 1823 a geologist, William Buckland, unearthed what he considered to be the remains of a young woman whose bones had been impregnated with red ochre, resulting in the find being dubbed the Red Lady of Paviland. The bones were later found to be those of a man about 25 years of age. Although his skull, vertebrae and right extremities were missing, it was estimated that he would have been about 5ft. 5ins. to 5ft. 8ins. tall with a build similar to the Cro-Magnon man found in southern France. He had been buried in the cave earth and covered with red ochre, which seems to have been a characteristic of early *Homo sapiens*, particularly those associated with the Aurignacian Culture. A number of artefacts were found near the remains, but none of them, due to a lack of archaeological techniques at the time of discovery, can be confidently connected with what was obviously a ceremonial burial. Failure to observe the stratigraphy meant that nothing could be dated except by comparison with similar finds elsewhere. However, with the help of carbon-14 dating, which measures the amount of residual carbon in organic matter such as wood or bone, we now have a fairly accurate date as to when the young man died—about 25,650 B.C.—which again links him to a late phase in the Aurignacian culture.

As has been said, early *Homo sapiens* were big game hunters, and the people who buried the young man at Paviland were not only showing respect for the dead, but were observing a burial ritual. The fact that they were living in a cold environment leads us to postulate that they wore skins similar to those worn by Eskimos. They also wore ornamentation as evidenced by an ivory pendant made from a diseased tusk found in the cave. In conclusion it may be assumed that the successive cultures of these early *Homo sapiens* were similar to that of certain North American Indians before the arrival of European settlers.

The Dawn of a New Age

The period 13,000-8,000 B.C. is often referred to as the Late Glacial—a mini-ice age of short duration—in which a glacier originating in the Brecon Beacons crept southwards, covering more than half the Gower Peninsula, advancing as far as the southern slopes of Cefn Bryn, at the same time obliterating all trace of earlier glaciations. During the later part of this period (after 9,000 B.C.) the ice retreated, the sea level started to rise and forests of birch and pine began to replace the tundra; by then, large animals such as the mammoth and the woolly rhinoceros had became extinct in Britain.

Creswellian Man

Between 10-8,000 B.C. the *Homo sapiens* of Britain developed a new industry in stone—the Creswellian industry—that was different from the one developed by their European counterparts. Examples of this British industry have been found at Paviland, but a more interesting Creswellian site has been found in what is now a secluded valley north of the village of Parkmill.

Cathole

Unlike Paviland, which is dangerous to access, Cathole can be reached quite easily. Located in a low cliff above Green Cwm, about 200m. beyond a restored megalithic tomb and hidden 15m. up in the wooded slope to the right, Cathole is one cave that provides an example of what Paviland must have looked like before the sea washed away an earlier coastline. Creswellian man would have occupied the mouth of Cathole, not the dank interior. The tasks that needed to be done to survive were carried out on the platform surrounding the cave entrance. Indeed, it is quite likely that the platform was enclosed by a palisade to give protection against wild animals such as the large cave bears that may have wandered into this secluded valley. Sat upon a log and clad in fur-lined clothes, Creswellian man certainly did his flint knapping on the platform outside the cave, for this is where excavators found a little of his workmanship—131 flakes and fragments, of which 18 finds were tools.

Cathole Cave, occupied in the Mesolithic period and later.

Cathole Cave, viewed from the inside.

Mesolithic Man: hunter-gatherer of the forests

The Mesolithic, or Middle Stone Age, began in Britain about 8,000 B.C. and continued to the 5th millennium B.C., by which time Britain had become an island. The southern coastline of Gower may not have extended far beyond what are now jagged rocks, but there was no Swansea Bay and no Carmarthen Bay. A man could walk more or less in a straight line from what is now Porthcawl to Mumbles Head, and from Rhosili to Caldey Island in Pembrokeshire.

A steady improvement in the climate encouraged the growth of trees, so much so that, by 6,500 B.C., Gower and its low-lying environs were either marshland or woodland with a canopy so high up that movement on the forest floor was relatively unhindered, the more so if underbrush had been burnt to make it easier to hunt game, which is what the Red Indians are believed to have done on the west coast of America. Mesolithic man, then, became a hunter-gatherer of the woods, no longer dependant on meat alone, but supplementing his diet with nuts and berries. This changing environment led to the disappearance of cave bears, cave lions, cave hyenas and probably the Irish elk. The huge herds of reindeer and European bison moved north, leaving red and roe deer to multiply in the expanding forests. The availability of smaller game may have been a factor in Mesolithic man's choice of tools. His industry differs from previous ones in that it comprises mainly of minutely worked flints, produced to meet a requirement for arrowheads.

Mesolithic man certainly made use of Paviland and Cathole, judging by the small number of microliths found at these sites, but he, like his Palaeolithic predecessors, must have made use of other forms of shelter, a fact that becomes apparent when the chipping site on Burry Holms is considered. On this island, which in Mesolithic times would have been a hill overlooking low-lying plains, a chipping site was located above a low cliff. There are no caves on the island, so the flint knapper and his kindred group must have erected some sort of shelter, using skins and poles which could be moved about at will, although the fact that early and late forms of implements have been found on the island suggests that the location may have been favoured by Mesolithic man over many centuries, if not millennia.

As a hilltop settlement Burry Holms may reflect Mesolithic man's apparent preference for elevated sites, for many Gower find spots are located in or near the cliffs on the south and west coast. It is not known whether he inhabited the low-lying forest that surrounded the Gower plateau, and whether he made use of rivers and the sea to fish and collect shellfish. However, it is known from the animal bones found at settlement sites elsewhere, notably in England, that Mesolithic hunter-gatherers feasted on both red and roe deer, on elk, wild pig and wild ox; dogs may have been used for hunting.

Neolithic Man: immigrant farmers in search of fertile soil

From about 5,800 B.C. onwards the climate gradually became quite warm, the temperature rising to as much as $2^1/_2$ degrees above what it is today. The growth of trees led to the development of fertile soil, ideal for farming, and in the 5th millennium B.C. the first farmers set foot in Gower. They probably came from the south-west of England. Those who came by boat may have done so in curraghs—made from withies and hides and propelled by oars—in which case their possessions, including grain and livestock, all had to be ferried across what would have then been a relatively narrow stretch of water. Those who journeyed overland, using the coastal lowlands, may have travelled at a leisurely pace, moving from one place to another each time the soil in their forest clearings lost its fertility, for they are unlikely to have known about fertilizers and crop rotation.

Whichever way they came, the newcomers may have found the fertile, lightly wooded plateau far more favourable for growing crops than the coastal lowlands, which are likely to have been heavily forested and probably waterlogged. The remains of submerged forests; that is, layers of peat carrying roots of oak and hazel, have been observed at low tide in Swansea Bay (between Singleton Park and Oystermouth), Port Eynon Bay and Broughton Bay.

These first farmers ushered in the Neolithic Period—the New Stone Age—and their technology in stone differs from the hunter-gatherers who continued to occupy the land. The Neolithic farmers still required flint or chert with which to make scrapers and knives, and their distinctive leaf-shaped arrowheads are identifiable to the trained eye, but what makes their stone industry unique are their polished, stone axe-heads.

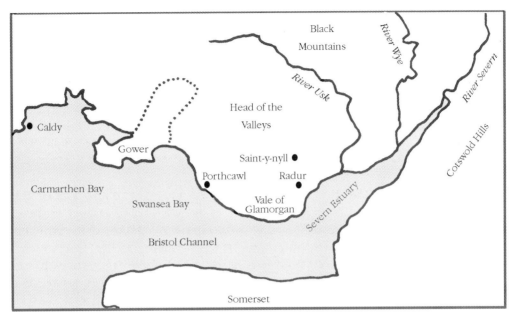

South-east Wales in the Prehistoric period.

When Neolithic man arrived in Gower he probably brought with him large flint axes for clearing trees and vegetation. In time he was obliged to trade for axes made from quarried stone and rubbed smooth. Several polished axe-heads have been found in Gower, originating from as far afield as Pembrokeshire, North Wales and Cornwall.

It has been proved that stone axes were effective tools, and once a section of woodland had been cleared, crops would be sown—emmer wheat, einkorn or barley—and the immigrants would stay in a suitable location until natural fertility had been exhausted, after which they would move on, repeating the process elsewhere. It is unfortunate that, apart from axes, all we have to show for early agriculture in Gower is the saddle quern found on Worm's Head.

It is assumed that mixed farming took place, for bones unearthed at Neolithic sites elsewhere show that these people kept cattle, pigs, goats and possibly sheep, the remains of goats/sheep being found in greater numbers than the remains of cattle. Hunting still provided additional meat as evidenced by the frequency with which arrowheads have been found. The type of game found in association with Neolithic artefacts are wild ox and roe deer, but red deer are also likely to have been hunted, and a pair of antlers with 16 points was recovered from peat many years ago when the construction of Swansea Docks was in progress.

Unlike their predecessors these early farmers made use of pottery, usually bowls that were deep, round-bottomed, with out-turned rims around the mouth, the upper edge either grooved or fluted. The remains of Neolithic pottery have been found in association with a hearth beneath a ring-cairn on Cefn Bryn, suggesting that a hut had once stood there—but what kind of hut?

The nearest example of a Neolithic hut was found beneath a burial mound on Newton Down, Porthcawl. A dry-stone wall, surviving in places to a height of 0.3m., marked the outline of a roughly rectangular building some 6m. long by 3m. wide, the walls surrounded on the outside by a clay bank. Three internal post-holes suggest that the hut carried a ridge roof; two more post-holes point to the existence of a doorway in the north wall. The artefacts found at this site imply that the hut had been occupied briefly during the 3rd millennium B.C. A single hut such as this gives the impression that Neolithic man lived in scattered farmsteads, although it is possible that the hut may have been one of several in a village that has left no other trace.

Neolithic man had his beliefs and in Gower he may have practised religious rituals at what appears to have been a henge monument at Newton, Rhosili. Nothing is visible on the ground, but an aerial photograph shows that a ditch had enclosed a circular area about 40m. in diameter. Two or three dark spots point to the presence of a ring of pits inside the enclosure. Monuments such as this, which may have been enhanced by rings of timber posts, are believed to have preceded the more elaborate ones such as Stonehenge.

Megalithic Tombs

From the 3rd millennium B.C. onwards the Neolithic people of Gower were expressing other aspects of their beliefs in earth and stone. Monumental stone chambers, some with passageways, were built and partially buried under mounds of earth or stones. It has been suggested that these megalithic tombs were not built for the benefit of an aristocracy, but that they were somehow connected with the worship of ancestors. If this is true, then the people who built these tombs must have seen themselves as belonging to kindred groups, governed perhaps by elders. It is possible that religious ceremonies took place at the entrances of these tombs.

The *Royal Commission on Ancient and Historic Monuments in Glamorgan (RCAHM)* (Vol. I, Part I) lists six megalithic tombs in the Peninsula. The two most easterly tombs belong to the Severn-Cotswold group, their shared characteristics being a stone chamber or chambers at one end of a long mound. It is not known whether the practice of communal burial came to Gower as part of a folk movement, or even a religious movement, but Severn-Cotswold type tombs appear to have originated on the western seaboard of France, the movement arriving in Britain via the Bristol Channel to take root in the Cotswolds and the Black Mountains area of Brecknock. The movement also became established in the Vale of Glamorgan and in Gower as a result of independent landfalls.

Of the two Severn-Cotswold tombs sited in Gower, one can be found among the sand dunes of Penmaen Burrows. Its surviving chambers are in a damaged state and any associated mound may be buried under the huge dune to the west. The other tomb, known as Giant's Grave, has been restored, except for a roof, and is reached by an easy walk from Parkmill. The wedge-shaped mound of Giant's Grave is made of limestone rubble—not earth. Entry into this tomb is by way of a bell-shaped forecourt,

Giant's Grave, near Parkmill, a restored Severn-Cotswold chambered long cairn.

leading to a gallery which gives access to four chambers. The tomb is dated to around 2,500 B.C. Apart from shards of Neolithic pottery, the skeletal remains of 20 to 24 persons, three of them children, were found in the chambers, all of them in a disturbed condition.

It has been claimed that interment in these tombs took place long after the bodies had been allowed to decompose elsewhere, and that the bones were, then, deposited in the chambers; hence their disturbed condition. What has been noted is that many skeletal remains have certain parts missing, such as skulls, and the inference is that these parts were removed for use in religious ceremonies. It has long been established that the people interred were short with longish heads. They were probably swarthy with (dark) curly hair, for that is how the people of south-east Wales were similarly described in both Roman and Anglo-Norman times.

The three most westerly tombs in the Peninsula have affinities with those in West Wales and Ireland. Their proximity to the Severn-Cotswold tombs provide an early example of Gower's position as a frontier zone between two regional cultures—that of West Wales, which displays a strong Irish influence, and that of south-east Wales, which has strong ties with the south-west of England. The two tombs known as Sweyn's Howes are close together on the lower, eastern slope of Rhosili Down. Both tombs are in a ruinous state, but the northern one is undoubtedly a portal dolmen; that is, three upright slabs forming three sides of a square and supporting a capstone. Both appear to have been incorporated in mounds that, originally, may have been oval in shape.

The third member of the Western Group is Maen Ceti, better known as Arthur's Stone. This is a much more impressive monument. There is, however, disagreement over whether the huge capstone—originally weighing 30-35 tons until a portion broke

Maen Ceti/Arthur's Stone, Cefn Bryn, as seen from the north.

off—stands in a position designated by nature, or whether it was moved there by an early farming community so that it could be seen from the plains to the north. Whatever the truth, the builders dug under the stone and underpinned it with more than a dozen boulders to form two chambers. At an unknown date a portion of the great stone fell away to the west, possibly as a result of water finding its way into a crack and freezing. It is possible that the larger, remaining section then swivelled into its present position. Judging by the surrounding banks, the capstone may have been encompassed by a circular mound of stones which had a diameter of 23m.

The sixth megalithic tomb has been described as a chambered long cairn. Sited just below the steep, southern slope of Cefn Bryn, this is a long cairn with a central cist that may have a slight affinity with the Western Group of tombs. There is a possibility that a seventh tomb, described as the remains of a long cairn, existed at Upper Killay until it was obliterated to make way for two bungalows.

The Uplands Beyond Gower

Neolithic people, as has been said, were immigrant farmers who established themselves in the Peninsula over a long period of time. What, then, became of the Mesolithic hunter-gatherers? It is probable that, initially, both cultural groups lived side by side, but as time went by so the hunter-gatherers found themselves faced with a choice: either they adopted the ways of their Neolithic neighbours, as seems to have been the case in Ireland and in England, or they held onto their way of life and their language in coastal forests or in the upland region to the north which, at the time, was covered by almost limitless woodland.

To the north-east there is indisputable evidence that Mesolithic hunter-gatherers roamed the hills around the head of the Rhondda Valleys, and may have continued to do so long after the first farmers set foot in Gower, but by 3,000 B.C. the climate is believed to have been at its best, warmer and drier than it is today, and the forests that had formed during the post-glacial period certainly contributed to the soil becoming fertile even on the uplands. Favourable conditions such as this would have encouraged Neolithic farmers to expand into the upland regions where they could grow crops at a height of up to 300m. above sea level. Indeed, a megalithic tomb may have been built on a ridge north-west of Pontardawe, although there are many who would argue that the huge stones found there are not set out in a way that resembles those in the Peninsula. On the other hand, it could be an attempt by Mesolithic men to imitate the burial practices of their Neolithic neighbours.

The Beaker Folk

From about 2,500 B.C. onwards copper implements begin to appear in Europe, to be followed, from around 2,000 B.C., by implements made of a much harder alloy called bronze. Thus the dawn of a new age had arrived—the Bronze Age—and about this time a new people were making their presence known. Originating in Spain and Portugal, these people interred their dead not in communal tombs, but buried them individually, laying the corpse on its left side in a flexed position. Sometimes the corpse would be placed in a stone cist, sometimes a shallow pit, with or without a covering mound or earth (a barrow) or stones (a cairn).

Buried with the dead was a distinctive type of pottery—a beaker—which probably contained a farewell meal. The beaker itself has prompted some archaeologists to refer to these people as the Beaker Folk. What is remarkable about them is that their skeletons show that, unlike their Neolithic neighbours, they were robust, rugged-featured with broad skulls that were frequently flat at the back, not unlike the people of Upper Palaeolithic times. These people were accomplished archers, judging by their finely-worked flint arrowheads and the archery equipment that has been found in their graves; their copper daggers show that they were acquainted with metallurgy.

It is assumed that the Beaker Folk were nomadic herdsmen, which helps explain their migratory character. The fact that, for centuries, they did not interbreed with the Neolithic people whom they came into contact with makes it possible to follow their movements. They migrated throughout west and central Europe, entering Britain via the south coast to spread out in all directions, some making for Salisbury Plain were they had a hand in building one phase of Stonehenge. They entered south-east Wales by several overland routes where they flourished from about 2,000 B.C. onwards.

Evidence for a Beaker Folk presence in Gower rests upon the meagre finds at two sites, one being Spritsail Tor where fragments of a beaker were found in a midden—a midden in this instance being a refuse dump near a vanished dwelling. At the other end of the Peninsula, on Colts Hill, Oystermouth, a barrow yielded fragments of another beaker in connection with a hearth and post-holes which showed that part of a round hut, estimated to be 9m. in diameter, had been buried under the barrow. The fragments here, as at Spritsail Tor, represent a late stage in the evolution of beaker ware; those at

Oystermouth are of such a debased character as to suggest that the hut had been built at a time when the Beaker Folk were at last merging with their Neolithic neighbours.

The Neolithic People of the Early Bronze Age

Throughout the period 2,000 to 1,500 B.C. the Beaker Folk were just one of many cultural groups in Britain because their Neolithic neighbours were by no means homogenous, at least, not in respect of their burial rites. Megalithic tombs were no longer in vogue, but in Gower communal burial continued to be practised by at least one small community, for at Tooth Cave (not far from Giant's Grave) the bones of eight individuals were found, all placed in a manner suggesting that the bodies had been allowed to decompose elsewhere. The bones were discovered in association with stone implements of Early Bronze Age date. This may not, however, be an isolated example of how Neolithic people continued the practice of communal burial. There are many caves and fissures in Gower that have yielded human remains. Unfortunately, none of them can be precisely dated.

Elsewhere the Neolithic population had gone over to cremating their dead, placing the burnt bones and ash in cists or pits that were, then, buried beneath barrows or cairns. Sometimes a bucket-shaped food-vessel would be placed in the grave; fragments of one such vessel were found beneath the barrow on Colts Hill, Oystermouth. There were, however, several types of cinerary urns made to contain burnt bones and ash, the most common in Gower being the collared-rim urns, formally known as overhanging-rim urns, and these may reflect differences among the communities which cremated their dead. Perhaps the best indicators to different cultural groups within the indigenous Neolithic population are to be found in the form of the mounds which covered their pits and cists.

Cairns and Barrows

Before concentrating on the burial mounds which dot the Gower landscape we should, first, expand our horizons and consider an extension of the Gower Peninsula. We need to do this in order to compare the different spheres of lowlands and uplands that determine Welsh history. The more fertile lowlands, to which the Peninsula belongs, became home to intrusive, often invasive cultures, whereas the not-so-prosperous uplands lent itself to the survival of long-established native cultures. The Gower we need to consider, then, is the Medieval lordship of that same name, the bounds of which encompassed not only the Peninsula, but the mountainous hinterland to the north, between the Loughor and Tawe Rivers, and also the Medieval appendage of Kilvey on the east bank of the Tawe River.

The *RCAHM,* (Vol. I, Part I) lists 119 cairns and barrows within what was once the Medieval Lordship of Gower; that is, with the exception of a small area in the north-west corner. Most of these ancient monuments are confined to two areas, one being the western half of the Peninsula where three ridges have the following concentrations—Cefn Bryn 33 sites, Rhosili Down 14, Llanmadog Hill 13. The other concentra-

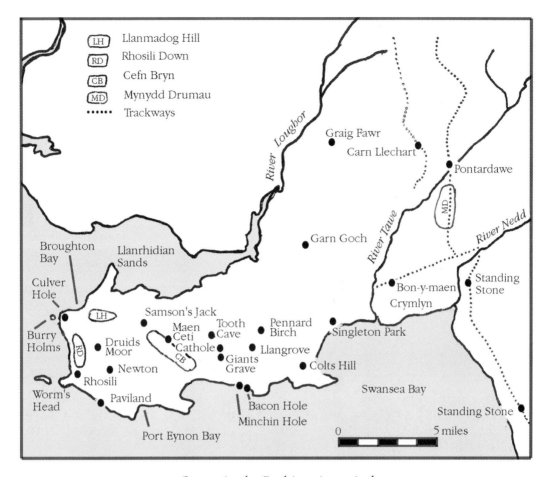

Gower in the Prehistoric period.

tion is near Pontardawe where 26 cairns are sited on four ridges. There is also a small concentration of seven cairns on Graig Fawr, north-east of Pontardulais. There appears to be a preference for ridges, but it must be said that barrows sited on what is now good agricultural land may have been ploughed out centuries ago.

The vast majority of the monuments are cairns—stone being readily available at most locations—and these have either been reduced to a spread of stones, or their cists and pits have been rifled by robbers and antiquarians who left cairns looking like craters. Only six monuments have been excavated by archaeologists who knew what they were doing. Further statistics are as follows: 86 monuments are either round or oval-shaped mounds, 27 are classified as ring-cairns and six are platform-cairns. A platform-cairn is a circular, slightly raised, level area of stones, often kerbed, with a cist or pit near the centre; one of the six has a superimposed cairn on top of it. By contrast a ring-cairn can be described as a roughly circular space enclosed by upright slabs, or more often than not by a bank of earth or stones. Some are associated with collared-

Cairn near Arthur's Stone on Cefn Bryn.

rim urns, some display the remains of cists, some appear to have had a purely ritual purpose, while others defy definition and may have nothing to do with the Early Bronze Age. One of the most imposing ring-cairns in its day was that of Carn Llechart, sited on a ridge north-west of Pontardawe. Here, a circular area, about 14m. in diameter, is enclosed by a ring of 25 upright slabs. At the centre of the internal space is a rifled cist. The grave robbers have left no clues as to who built this monument. All that can be said of it now is that it reflects the importance of stone circles.

On Graig Fawr two closely-set circular banks are separated by a depression that has been formed by scraping away the original surface between the banks. A causeway on the north-east gives access to an enclosed space with a diameter of about 40m., within which is a small enclosure set against the inner bank. The monument bears a resemblance to circles in West Wales and Ireland, and there is one in Lancashire where the inner enclosure concealed what remained of a ring of posts, a cremation burial and funerary ware. It seems that this particular circle may have had a ritual function, its denuded remains masking the mysterious rituals of a truly mystic people, the same people who built Avebury and Stonehenge.

The majority of ring cairns are relatively small, the central areas enclosed by a bank of rubble in which there is an entrance and sometimes the suggestion of a cist. In 1982 excavators got to work on one such ring-cairn on Cefn Bryn. There was no burial in the cairn, negative evidence that suggests its function may have been purely ritual. The entrance of the cairn had been deliberately blocked up at a later date and the interior filled with stones as if to make the point that it had gone out of use. Could it be that this cairn had been an arena for family rituals?

Whatever their purpose, ring-cairns have been found buried beneath barrows and cairns. One of the best examples of this comes from a barrow known as Pennard Burch. In 1941, prior to its destruction to make way for a wartime airfield on Fairwood Common, the huge barrow revealed there had been several stages to its construction.

A cist, containing a primary cremation in association with fragments of a collared-rim urn, had been enclosed by a small ring-cairn. A pyre, comprising of oak branches, had been fired over the cist which, in turn, had been covered by a mound of clay. The clay mound had been enlarged with an additional covering of turf, and the outer rim surrounded by a second ring of stones. A final outer covering of clay resulted in a barrow measuring 23m. in diameter. It is possible that the enlargement was due to people at a later date making use of an existing barrow, although no secondary burials were found in the outer layers.

Other large barrows in Gower have proved to be small graveyards. A cairn on Mynydd Garn Goch, for example, had at least nine secondary burials, yielded seven cists, nine cinerary urns (two of them collared-rim), three pigmy cups, as well as charcoal, flints and animal bones. Here again there had been a primary burial inside a buried ring-cairn. The body of the cairn is said to have been a mound of earth, 27.4m .in diameter, topped with *a huge pile of stones*, giving it a total height of over 3m. Little of the cairn remains today.

An Early Bronze Age Settlement

In the Vale of Glamorgan, barrows that have been systematically excavated have revealed that a great deal of ritual accompanied cremation burials. Occasionally pigmy cups – which may have served as incense vessels—were placed inside the urns. Often a house was buried beneath the mound, preserving a glimpse of how the dead once lived. A barrow at Saint-y-nyll, near Cardiff, contained the ashes of a woman and child, their remains placed in a central pit and covered with a stone slab, but a surprise lay in store for the excavators when, stripping the mound to ground level, they discovered three oval huts had once occupied the site.

The southernmost hut had been built first, to be superseded by a hut to the north-east, the post-holes of which showed signs that the posts had been replaced. The shallow channels linking the peripheral post-holes of that hut indicated where a wickerwork wall had once stood. Between the remains of these two huts were the post-holes of the largest hut, its oval-shape measuring between 3.7 and 4.6m.; this hut, or at least its framework, may have been still standing when it was buried beneath the barrow. Of the 500 animal bones found on site sheep were the most numerous, outnumbering cattle by four to one. Wild boar was also well represented, and there were three claws of a brown bear.

Most of the pottery fragments were from collared-rim urns. A few shards of hemispherical bowls were of secondary Neolithic tradition. Flint implements and fragments helped to complete a picture of an Early Bronze Age farmstead that had been sited on the crest of a low ridge, one where a succession of huts were built and then abandoned when the materials used in their construction began to rot. At another barrow in the Vale of Glamorgan charred grains of wheat and barley show the kind of cereal cultivated at about the same time.

Enlarged Burial Mounds, Standing Stones and Trackways

Before the end of the Early Bronze Age the Beaker Folk had lost their identity and merged with their Neolithic neighbours, the practice of cremation everywhere prevailing. In Gower the only apparent change seems to have been a move towards bigger burial mounds which, in the case of Pennard Burch and Bishopston Burch are believed to have been enlargements of existing burial mounds, using turf taken from the surrounding fields, into which secondary burials were probably inserted; to these we may add Garn Goch and perhaps those exceptionally large cairns on Cefn Bryn, Rhosili Down and Llanmadog Hill.

One phenomenon that is ascribed to the Early Bronze Age (and later) is the Standing Stone, in Welsh the *meini hirion*. Some of these unhewn monoliths originally stood to a height of 4m., like the leaning *meini hirion* on Cefn Gwyrd, a ridge to the north of Pontardawe. Much has been written about the energy field around these stones and their association with pagan rituals, although no one can really explain their true purpose. Cremation deposits have been found under two stones in the Vale of Glamorgan, which suggests that either the stones were put there to commemorate the dead, or sacrifices had been carried out to consecrate the stones. Other excavations in the holes from which stones have fallen have produced negative results.

Some stones appear to be connected with ancient trackways. One such trackway,

Samson's Jack, a standing stone near Weobley Castle.

in association with ten stones, is said to have passed through the Vale of Glamorgan, skirted Swansea Bay, and crossed the River Nedd at Neath to continue in a south-westerly direction till it reached the stone at Bon-y-maen; from there the trackway may have met the Tawe River at a point where, centuries later, the Romans constructed a ford. A more convincing trackway, flanked by two stones and seven cairns, may have led from the ford at Neath, over Mynydd Drumau to descend to a ford at or near Pontardawe, beyond which it led over Cefn Gwryd to become lost in the landscape to the north. A second trackway further west, over Mynydd Carnllechart, has four cairns close to it and probably led to the Llandovery area.

In Gower there is a concentration of stones between Stout Hall and Oldwalls, all of them sited below the western end of Cefn Bryn. Eight of these stones are extant and there are records of another two. At Burry, three stones were originally placed in a straight line, a not unusual arrangement. Further north, in the fields west of Oldwalls, is Samson's Jack, the tallest surviving stone in the concentration, standing 3.2m. high. Records refer to a second concentration of six or seven stones below the western end of Llanmadog Hill, all of them now lost. There are also at least 15 field-names in the Peninsula which point to the presence of stones now lost—Long Stone, Hoar Stone and Stone Field to name but a few.

The Middle Bronze Age 1,500-1,000 B.C.

What really defines this period is the appearance of a new range of bronze weapons— socketed spearheads, daggers, dirks, swords and above all palstaves (slim-bodied axe-heads)—that are easily identified and made from a mixture of copper and a small amount of lead. The number of weapons found may reflect the growth of a warrior class. In Wessex—meaning southern England, particularly the western half centred on Salisbury Plain—hillside and hilltop settlements begin to appear about this time, some of them defended by palisades, with or without banks and ditches, a reflection of growing insecurity.

The Middle Bronze Age experienced periods of increased rainfall that had a detri-mental effect on the land, the soil on the populated ridgetops becoming leached to produce coarse moor grass, the still forested valleys becoming extremely damp. This may have led to the people of upland Gower drifting towards the fertile lowlands, a move exacerbated by the arrival of people from beyond the borders of Gower, all of them in search of land. It is pressure such as this that probably led to the old pattern of life eventually giving way to one in which bands of warriors were dictating the terms. The tradition of communal gatherings at stone circles and the like went into decline; in the new order the emphasis would eventually be on defence.

To a large extent our knowledge of the Middle Bronze Age is dependant upon chance finds or hoards, like the remarkable bronze sword found at Oystermouth, or the hoard of bronze palstaves discovered at Llanmadog. Sometimes a find has an air of mystery about it, like the palstave found beside the knee of an extended skeleton in the Crymlyn Burrows. *'Was this a burial?'* we may wonder. Or did the man fall in a skirmish, his right hand still grasping the handle of a palstave, his wooden shield soon to rot in the marsh where he fell?

A most remarkable discovery is the hoard of scrap-metal found under a flat stone at Langrove in the parish of Pennard. We can assume that this hoard, consisting of what remained of three swords, a socketed spearhead, a socketed axe-head and a barbed and tanged arrowhead, had been the property of a smith whose intention may have been to hide it until he was ready to melt it down and refashion it, but who may have met an untimely death. What is remarkable about the hoard is the composition of many of the bronze objects—copper with a little arsenic, nickel and cobalt. It is not known where the hoard originated, but its discovery in 1827 led to Pennard becoming the adopted name of an industry that flourished throughout southern Britain and in France during this period.

There can be no doubt that the warrior class was also the wealthiest. Not only could the men within it afford bronze weapons, but they also wore ornamentation in gold as well as bronze. A gold, Tara-type torc was found at an unknown location on Gower's northern border, indisputable evidence of a privileged class, which means there must have been a servile class of slaves and serfs, one that greatly outnumbered the first, and probably originated from communities that were overrun by warlords and their retinues.

In Wessex, where the evidence for a warrior aristocracy is irrefutable, the ashes of the dead were placed in a new type of urn—the Wessex-biconical—and deposited in cemeteries which archaeologists call urnfields. The people who are associated with the Urnfield Culture appear to have spread northwards, possibly by conquest, to establish themselves in Shropshire and North Wales, where their urnfields and defended hilltop/hillside settlements have been found. No urnfields have been discovered in South Wales, but the very idea of cemeteries may have helped to promote another phenomenon which excavation has failed to resolve.

Cairn Cemeteries

Found in upland regions all over Britain and wherever stones are abundant, cairn cemeteries are groups of small, often shapeless cairns that defy definition. Even as far back as 1810 antiquarians were pondering on whether these heaps of stone were cairn cemeteries, or the result of land clearance for cultivation. It may be that the latter explanation should be applied to the majority of sites. The trouble is, some of the cairns within certain groups look like genuine burial mounds, displaying suggestions of damaged cists and kerbs.

In 1936 a disturbed cist in one so-called cemetery near Neath was examined, yielding a shard of Romano-British pottery. This did nothing to resolve unanswered questions, and the results of excavations at Welsh sites in 1941 and 1950 were in favour of the land clearance interpretation, although the 1950 excavation did yield more shards of what may have been Roman-British ware. Then rescue excavation at a cemetery in Glamorgan in 1981 showed that one unlikely looking cairn covered three pits, each containing burnt wood and bones. Radiocarbon dating assigned the cremations to the Early Bronze Age.

The *RCAHM* (Vol. I, Part I) lists three cairn cemeteries in Gower as probably sepulchral, all of them on or near ridges. Two are located in the uplands, and one can be found on Cefn Bryn, a little to the south-east of Arthur's Stone. The last mentioned cemetery is the largest with 38 cairns, two of which look like ring-cairns; the remaining mounds may be associated with early cultivation that is known to have taken place on this part of the ridge.

Culver Hole

One place where people were almost certainly buried during the Middle Bronze Age is Culver Hole, Llangenydd, a cave that nowadays is both difficult and dangerous to reach. In prehistoric times, when there would have been no danger of high tides swamping the interior, the cave had obviously been used as an ossuary over a long period of time. Among the many bones and artefacts found at Culver Hole were fragments of 11 bucket-like urns which resemble the Wessex-biconical urns of the Urnfield Culture. The remoteness of the site has lent itself to the idea that an immigrant community had established itself in the vicinity of the cave, one that had fled from a *coup d'état* in southern England.

Cooking Mounds

No Middle Bronze Age settlement sites have been found in Gower, but here is as good a place as any to consider an unusual way of boiling meat. A site would be selected near a source of water from which a channel allowed the water to enter a plank-lined trough, into which went raw meat. One or more fires were used to heat stones, which were, then, thrown or rolled into the trough, heating the water and eventually boiling the meat. When the trough had cooled, the burnt stones were taken from the trough and thrown some distance away; in time a mound of burnt stones would accumulate all round the cooking area, except where water had been channelled from a pond or stream. Thus a horseshoe-shaped ring-cairn of burnt stones provides the archaeologist with clues to identify the site as a cooking mound.

This method of boiling meat has been proved feasible and must have been used over a long period of time. A trough in Ireland, for instance, provided a radiocarbon date of 1760 B.C. plus or minus 270 years. At Radur, near Cardiff, an extremely large cooking mound yielded Iron Age pottery that may date to the first century A.D. Five cooking mounds have been identified in Gower, the most notable being the one on Druids Moor to the south of Hardings Down. Here a grass-grown mound with a dish-shaped centre measures 21m. in diameter. The mound opens out on the north-west where there is a pond from which water could have been drawn. Recent excavation has shown the mound to be made up of burnt stones and blackened earth. Somewhere nearby, the remains of a round hut may await discovery.

The Late Bronze Age 1,000-600 B.C.

An increase in rainfall during the Late Bronze Age has contributed to a lack of finds, the acid soil inhibiting the survival of organic material; moreover, the absence of burial structures has denied the archaeologist an important source of information, leaving him with only an abundance of bronze artefacts with which to piece together a picture of the times. The bronzes were the work of travelling smiths, the craftsmen who supplied the warrior, land-owning class with razors, sickles, cauldrons, weapons and also horse-harnesses and chariot fittings, evidence that, by the Late Bronze Age, horses were used in battle. Many of the finds in south-east Wales appear to have been brought over from Somerset, the raw material—the copper and the lead—coming mainly from the south-west of England. The weapon that appears to have been favoured most by the warriors of south-east Wales is the socket axe; its distribution seems to define a tribal area.

Gower has virtually nothing to show for this prehistoric equivalent of the Dark Ages. Yet a picture of society in those far-off days can still be created from the meagre evidence that comes from Britain as whole. The weapons tell us that the Late Bronze Age was an heroic age, one that, in Wales, endured well into historic times. This was an age when petty chieftains and their bellicose companions feasted in large, round huts. It is this sort of fraternity that may have promoted the growth of ruling dynasties as far back as the latter part of Early Bronze Age.

The *Clanna*

It is customary to think of a clan as a sub-division of a tribe, a group of people who claimed descent from a common ancestor, but clan is a modern term, originating from the Irish word *clanna*, meaning *children of*; that is, the descendants of a named person who founded a ruling dynasty. In other words a strong man laid claim to territory which he and his descendants ruled, the descendants being known as the *children of*. Outsiders may have looked upon the subject population as *so and so's* people, but they were not part of the *clanna* as, indeed, the citizens of the United Kingdom are not part of the royal family.

The oldest known founder of a *clanna* in Britain is said to have lived in Scotland during the 9th century A.D. That is recorded history, but ruling dynasties must have existed long before then, and as *clanna* is an Irish word it need hardly be said that ruling dynasties existed in Ireland as well. In the Gaelic world the dynasties died out as a result of Anglo-Norman conquest, except in the Scottish Highlands where the relationship between the *clanna* and the subject people changed. In the period between the 15th and 18th centuries A.D., the subject people were more closely aligned with their ruling dynasties, with the result that they also claimed to be the *children of* a distant ruler; that is the origin of the Highland clans.

Of course, a ruler and his descendants relied on the support of their companions-in-arms, and to ensure loyalty they had to be both tactful and generous, awarding their followers with gifts and, most important of all, land so that they became members of a land-holding nobility whose sons served as companions-in-arms to succeeding rulers. In Wales, where the attitude of free men had been modified by the fact that their forefathers had been Roman citizens and who, therefore, considered themselves to be of privileged stock, it was the free men who, in many respects, held the reins of power, for the records relating to the Middle Ages are full of occasions when they disposed of rulers who displeased them, or when the most influential of them usurped the power of a *clanna* in certain localities.

A New People

From about 600 B.C. onwards a new technology begins to appear in Gower, signifying the dawn of a new age—the Iron Age—and for the first time archaeologists have the name of a hitherto unknown people, a people who spread their culture and their language throughout the length and breadth of Europe—the Celts—a people who gave Wales its identity and its language, reason to devote a chapter to who these people were, where they came from and how they arrived in Gower.

CHAPTER II
Celts and Romans

How and when the Celts first appeared in Europe let alone Gower is a mystery. Their homeland appears to have been Central Europe from where they, or at least their culture, spread in all directions. Their artefacts have been found throughout Europe, from Scotland to Spain, from Ireland to Hungary; they have even been discovered in eastern Turkey.

Hallstatt

Archaeology provides the earliest evidence for the existence of Celts. The evidence comes from the distinctive, decorative art that adorns their vessels and metalwork—both bronze and iron. Undoubtedly, one of the most comprehensive examples of Celtic art comes from an Iron Age cemetery on a hill outside the Austrian village of Hallstatt where, from about 770 B.C. onwards, the aristocracy were buried with beautifully-decorated vessels, ornamented weaponry and horse trappings—artefacts that have served as examples to which finds from other parts of Europe have been compared, thereby confirming or denying their Celtic origin. In broad terms, the Hallstatt Culture—otherwise known as Iron Age A in Britain—began around 800 B.C. on the Continent, and persisted to as late as 300 B.C. in far-off Britain and Ireland.

La Tene

The name *La Tene* comes from a location at the eastern end of Lake Neuchâtel in Switzerland where, in 1858, the water level dropped to reveal blackened timbers and an abundance of artefacts of exceptional beauty and sophistication. These artefacts became the next great landmark in Celtic craftsmanship, being far more advanced than any of the Hallstatt finds; they gave rise to what archaeologists call the La Tene Culture—known also as Iron Age B in Britain—which began about 600 B.C. and reached its high point in the valleys of Austria and Bavaria and by the Lakes in Switzerland, only to be swamped by Roman civilization from the first century B.C. onwards. So how did objects associated with the Celts reach a place as remote as Gower?

A movement of Ideas

At one time it was believed that the Celts migrated in waves from their homeland, a succession of unstoppable warrior-migrants who where able to overwhelm the people of other cultures because their iron weapons were superior to anything made of stone or bronze. They were seen as a people who made use of ponies, their cavalrymen and charioteers terrifying all who stood in their way. Nowadays, archaeologists play down the notion of mass migrations and speak in terms of a movement of ideas in which non-Celtic people accepted the use of iron and, in doing so, adopted a distinctive form of art as a result of trade and itinerant craftsmen. Unlike the Romans, Celtic craftsmen had no regard for straight lines; they made use of leaves and tendrils, of animal shapes and the human head. They created *triskeles* (a figure with three legs radiating from a central point) and other identifiable patterns, all of which can be found in La Tene art; they were the attributes that were the basis of commonality, the white, foamy waves that stood out in a sea of regional differences.

Llyn Fawr

No cache of Iron Age artefacts has been found within the bounds of what was once the Medieval lordship of Gower, but a few miles from Gower's north-eastern border, in the small mountain lake of Llyn Fawr, near Hirwaun, 24 objects—21 of bronze, three of iron—were discovered in 1911, buried in peat. The iron objects are dated to around 600 B.C., a time when the Hallstatt phase of Iron Age Culture had only a toe-hold in Wales. The assemblage includes an iron sword, a harness and a socketed axe; among the bronze objects are two cauldrons, two sickles and a razor. The origins of the finds are diverse, coming from both the Continent and Ireland; a few may have been made in Glamorgan. Equally varied are the suggestions as to how the cache came to be deposited in a tarn. It may have been spoil taken in a long-distant raid—on the fertile Gower Peninsula perhaps—or the artefacts may have been placed in the tarn over a long period of time. Either way they were votive offerings to a pagan deity.

Iron Age Pottery 500 B.C. to 50 A.D.

Seldom found in South Wales, Iron Age A pottery has been discovered in two Gower caves—Culver Hole, near Llangenydd, and Bacon Hole, Pennard, the ware having links with the Hallstatt phase of Iron Age Culture. Shards of Iron Age B pottery, on the other hand, are relatively common and have been found at several Gower hill-forts and two caves. B ware has the form of deep, wide-mouthed bowls with out-turned rims, having a smooth, dark finish with little or no decoration, and may be connected with the arrival in South Wales of Continental influences, beginning about 300 B.C.

What the Early Historians had to say

All that has been written about the Celts from the 5th century B.C. to the time of Christ can be found in the works of their southern neighbours, the Romans and the Greeks, and it is from them that we learn of the movement of Celtic tribes or, more probably, of subdivisions which 'hived off' because of overpopulation, or because their northern neighbours, the Germans, put pressure on them to move. One writer, for example, records how a Gaulish king, burdened by an excess of people, dispatched two nephews with as many followers as they needed to overcome opposition. One nephew settled in Germany, the other in the Po Valley in Italy. The best known migrant group is the one that, in the 3rd century B.C., moved down through the Balkans and crossed over to Asia Minor (now Turkey) to become the Galatians to whom St. Paul wrote an epistle in the 1st century A.D. One classical writer described the Celts as:

> tall, their flesh moist and white, and not only is their hair naturally blond, but they enhance the colour by artificial means. Some shave, others cultivate a short beard; the nobles shave their cheeks, but allow a moustache to grow freely so that it covers their mouth to the extent that food gets entangled in the hairs, and when they drink, the liquid passes, as it were, through a sieve. They do not sit on chairs, but on the skins of wolves and dogs. Their meals are served by their youngest grown-up children, both boys and girls. They sit beside blazing fires where there are spits and cauldrons containing large pieces of meat.

The same writer states:

> they invite strangers to their feasts, and only when the meal is at an end do they ask who their guests are and what they are in need of. At dinner they are moved by chance remarks to disputes and, after a challenge, fight in single combat with little regard for their lives. They frequently exaggerate so as to extol themselves and diminish the status of others. They boast and threaten and are given to bombastic self-dramatization. Yet they are quick of mind with a natural ability for learning. They have poets whom they call 'Bards'. They sing to the accompaniment of instruments which resemble lyres. They also have philosophers and theologians whom they treat with special honour, whom they call 'Druids'.

Much of what has been said of the Celts by Classical writers was echoed in the 12th century A.D. by Gerald of Wales in his description of the Welsh. However, when the Roman historian, Tacitus, wrote about the tribesmen of south-east Wales he described them as dark-complexioned, usually with curly hair; from this it is obvious that the tall, blond Celts of Central Europe were not of the same stock as the inhabitants of South Wales, which serves to remind us that when we speak of Celts we speak of a culture, not a race.

The Celts of France and the Low Countries—known to the Romans as Gauls—were depicted as eager for war, depending upon their physique and upon their numbers for victory. Their aristocrats were well armed, their weapons consisting of a long sword worn on the right, a long shield, lengthy spears and the *mandaris*, a kind of javelin. Some of the people used bows and slings, and they had a wooden weapon, thrown by hand, with a range greater than that of arrows which they used for bird hunting as well as battle. They wore bronze helmets with large projections such as horns. Some wore chain-mail—a Celtic innovation—while others fought naked.

Horses

No description of the Celts would be complete unless there is at least a mention of their connection with ponies. Bronze and even iron horse trappings have been found in many Iron Age caches. The Celts were apparently such good horsemen that the Romans employed them as auxiliary troops. Gaulic cavalry served under Caesar during his invasions of Britain in 55 and 54 B.C. and, in the Claudian invasion of 43 A.D., Gaulic cavalry units are believed to have been in the forefront when it came to crossing rivers. It is not surprising, therefore, that one of the first auxiliary units to be raised in Britain appears to have been a cavalry formation, the *Ala Britannica*—but the Celts proved themselves to be more than just good horsemen.

In the aristocratic burial mounds of the Celtic world the remains of chariots are often found. These two-wheeled vehicles were of light construction—anything heavy would have been useless for travelling at speed over boggy and bumpy ground. Chariots were manned by two men whose purpose was to harass the enemy, discharging missiles, the noise of hooves and chariot wheels unnerving their opponents. At the time of Caesar's Gaulic wars, chariots were apparently no longer in use on the Continent, but towards the end of his second invasion of Britain he had to contend with the hit and run tactics of 4,000 British charioteers; shock troops such as these were reported to have been in action in Kent during the Claudian invasion of 43 A.D.

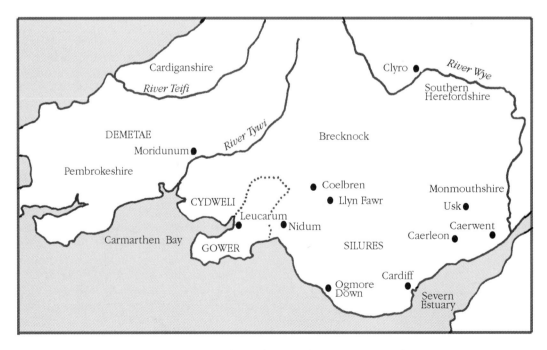

South Wales in the Celtic and Roman periods.

Hill-forts

Fortunately for the Greeks and the Romans the Celts spent more time raiding one another's territory than plundering their southern neighbours; hence the profusion of so-called hill-forts in Celtic territory. The *RCAHM (Glam.)* lists no less than 37 so-called hill-forts and related structures within the bounds of Medieval Gower, almost all of them sited in lowland situations. Not all hill-forts are necessarily a product of Iron Age society: some, like the three small, stone-walled cashels near Llangenydd, resemble the *llanau* which surrounded the early Christian monasteries; two very small enclosures with closely-set multiple banks and ditches may be the remains of 12th century Anglo-Norman castles. What is noticeable about the remaining hill-forts is their size in relation to the number of people who probably lived in them—It is as if the builders were more concerned with corralling cattle, which fits the belief that cattle raiding was prevalent among the Celts. With the exception of Cil Ifor Top, near Llanrhidian, which may have been a fortified village, all the hill-forts were probably defended farmsteads, the property of a land-holding aristocracy, though not all the forts would have been occupied simultaneously.

A good example of a small, Iron Age hill-fort is Hardings Down West, which occupies a spur at the western end of a small hill near Llangenydd. Its main defences consist of a bank and external ditch, enclosing an oval area of 1½ acres. No post-holes were found in the bank during excavation in 1962, yet it must have carried a palisade (or a box-like frame) and this, coupled with a 5m. drop to the bottom of the ditch, would have been a real obstacle for cattle thieves. To the south-east are two outer ramparts, neither of which continues round in a full circle. When excavated, a gap in the main rampart proved to carry four post-holes and a cobbled entrance passage. Three hut-platforms lay in the enclosure. The one to the north-west had been occupied by a round hut 7m. in diameter, the roof apparently supported by six or seven posts set in an oval. Shards of Iron Age B pottery were found on the floor. The larger platform near the centre of the enclosure revealed two periods of constructions, the earlier one a round hut, 10m. in diameter, with four huge posts set in a square. The floor of the third hut-platform was not cleared.

This particular type of hill-fort is listed in the *RCAHM* as a 'small fort with wide-spaced ramparts', and there were 11 of them in Gower. In many instances the wide spaces between the ramparts were probably used for

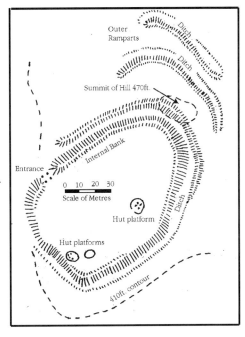

Hardings Down West Camp.

Banks and ditches of the Hardings Down West hill-fort.

corralling livestock. Some forts, like the one described above, appear to be unfinished, but it may be that the outer ramparts were sited between natural obstacles such as woods. It is possible that Hardings Down West may have originally been a univallate fort—meaning only one rampart surrounded the enclosed area—and that the outer ramparts were constructed at a later date. There are 18 univallate forts in Gower, almost all of them quite small. Both the univallate forts and the ones with wide-spaced, multiple ramparts are common throughout south-east Wales, West Wales, Cornwall, Devon and west Somerset, which suggest there may have been a cultural affinity among the natives on both sides of the Bristol Channel.

Although no undefended hut-settlements have been found in Gower, it is likely that they did exist, taking the form, perhaps, of several round huts linked by wicker fencing, home to a servile population. In recent years undefended settlements of Iron Age date have been found to be common enough in southern England.

Literacy and Language

The Celtic language was as widespread as *La Tene* art. We know this to be so because the Celts were not illiterate and Julius Caesar himself informs us that, while the Druids would not commit their teachings to writing, for most other purposes, such as public and private accounts, the Gauls used the Greek alphabet. Scattered Celtic inscriptions have been found in Spain, France, northern Italy and Turkey and these inscriptions date from the 4th century B.C. onwards. Further evidence comes from the legends on

Celtic coins (in Britain they used the Latin alphabet). What is interesting is that the language of the British Celts bore a strong resemblance to the extinct Gaulish language of ancient France; moreover, it is assumed that in the 1st century A.D. the majority of the population in Britain spoke in the Celtic tongue, and that in remote and difficult places, such as Wales and the North, there were pockets where other ancient languages continued to be spoken.

An Intractable Tribe

It can safely be assumed that, by the 1st century A.D., Gower shared a cultural affinity with people on both sides of the Bristol Channel, but its links with affiliations such as a tribe are difficult to determine. Under Roman rule South Wales appears to have been divided into two tribal areas. Little is known of the people of West Wales other than Roman forts suggest that, initially, they resisted Roman rule and that by the 5th century they were referred to as the Demetae, but according to the Roman historian, Tacitus, the people who occupied south-east Wales in the late 1st century A.D. were the Silures, whom he described as swarthy, usually with (dark) curly hair. Their appearance and the fact that, in his mind, South Wales lay opposite Spain led him to believe that Spain was where they came from. However, the archaeological evidence does not support such a hypothesis. At best the artefacts hints at trade contacts with north-west France. Whatever their origin, it is possible that the Silures came to south-east Wales in small groups over a long period of time, their leaders bent on usurping the possessions of the Bronze Age dynasties in the plains of the pre-1974 County of Monmouthshire, the Vale of Glamorgan and the Gower Peninsula, then gradually extending their control over the upland regions like the Anglo-Normans did during the Medieval period, the result being two cultures existing side by side until the culture and language of the Silures predominated. Of course, it is not known whether the language of the Silures had been Celtic, it can only be presumed that it was so, for Classical historians never mentioned what languages were spoken by the natives of Britain let alone south-east Wales. A native language only begins to appear in written form in the late 6th century A.D., and that language (with an admixture of words borrowed from the Romans) was an early form of Welsh.

Tacitus has nothing to say about the extent of Silurian territory, but the old County of Monmouthshire was certainly their heartland and, judging by their dogged resistance to the Romans, they must have been a large tribe, occupying perhaps parts of several pre-1974 counties—Gloucester, Hereford, Brecknock and Glamorgan with Gower possibly their most westerly locality. They were a people who do not appear to have had a king during the time of their resistance to Roman rule, for if they had had one, Tacitus would surely have informed us of his name. It can only be presumed that they were a federation of communities, each with its own *clanna*.

Thus the picture so far obtained is that the Celts came to Gower in small numbers over a long period of time, bringing with them all the hallmarks of their Iron Age Culture—but at this point let us pause for thought. If Iron Age Culture is synonymous with the Celts, then the Celts must have existed in Bronze Age times. Indeed, the Late Bronze Age has identifiable links with the Hallstatt phase of Iron Age Culture, for there were people in Late Bronze Age Wales using long, leaf-shaped swords and spears, who made use of ponies and lived in hill-forts; moreover, Late Bronze Age socketed axes abound in an area that coincides with the later tribal territory of the Silures. There is also one important factor that has not yet been considered.

Genes

Y-chromosomes are found only in men and, therefore, pass from father to son, only changing slowly over a long period of time. In an area extending from East Anglia to North Wales, samples of Y-chromosomes were recently taken from men whose grandfathers had been born in the same localities where the men lived. The result was that one group of chromosomes was found to be present in both England and Wales, but was far more common in Wales, becoming less so the further east one goes. Conversely, other groups were more common in East Anglia, becoming less so the further west one travels; moreover, the 'other groups' were even more common in northern Europe where the Anglo-Saxons and, later, the Vikings came from. An interesting finding about genes is that Welshmen have a biological identity that was set some 3,500 years ago, as far back as the beginning of the Middle Bronze Age in fact.

Burials

If there is one thing that exemplifies diversity among the Celts it is the way they buried their dead, the differences ranging from the lavish inhumations of Central Europe to the simple cremation cemeteries of south-east England. Throughout south-western Britain the normal practice appears to have been inhumation, but in South Wales there were differences according to status. For the lower classes their final resting place might be a rubbish pit, whereas warriors are known to have been buried in full regalia, like those found in a cemetery on Ogmore Down, where helmets encased two skulls and the remains of iron daggers and spearheads were found beside the bones. The storm-tossed cave of Culver Hole, Llangenydd, in Gower has yielded the disarticulated bones of more than forty individuals. They may not all belong to the Iron Age/Roman period, although Roman coins and other artefacts suggest that at least some of them do.

Before narrating the fierce resistance of the Silures to Roman rule, it is necessary to consider a third Iron Age Culture—Iron Age C—identified not by a more sophisticated form of craftsmanship, but by wheel-made pottery and the use of coins. The people who are associated with this culture are better known by what appears to be a tribal name.

The Belgae

When Julius Caesar subjugated Gaul between 59 and 52 B.C., he came into contact with a group of tribes called the Belgae which, he claimed, were descended from tribes which long ago had come from across the Rhine to settle in that part of Gaul which is now Belgium and northern France; elements of these tribes had also settled in southern Britain. When the Roman Emperor, Claudius, invaded Britain in A.D. 43 the tribes of southern Britain united under Togodumnus, King of the Catuvellauni (believed to have been a Belgic tribe) and his brother, Caratacus. The fighting was short-lived; the British were defeated, Togodumnus was slain and Caratacus fled west-wards, taking with him his family and, no doubt, a warband of loyal followers, where he continued to oppose the Romans for several years to come.

From the evidence that is available it would appear that Caratacus was not the only one to flee rather than submit to Roman rule. Belgic/Iron Age C pottery has been found in a number of hill-forts scattered throughout the plains of Monmouthshire and Glamorgan, whereas in Gower similar ware has been found in just one cave (Minchin Hole). It may be that some of the pottery had come to south-east Wales as a result of trade. It is also feasible that some of it may have been brought to the area by people who, like Caratacus, preferred to move rather than live under Roman rule.

The Silurian Wars

The Roman historian, Dio, provides the bare outlines of the Roman conquest of southern Britain in 43 A.D. Then the historian, Tacitus, leaps forward four years to inform us that in 47, the first Roman governor, Plautius, was succeeded by Ostorius Scapula and that the event was marked by an attack by tribes outside the Roman province of southern Britain, the attackers believing that the new governor would be unable to mount a counter-offensive due to the onset of winter. Tacitus does not point a finger at Caratacus, but many historians believe that the attack was instigated by him and involved at least one tribe from Wales. Scapula's response was to march at the head of several auxiliary cohorts and stamp out the opposition.

Auxiliaries were non-Romans, usually barbarians, recruited from conquered lands throughout the Empire, their reward for 25 years arduous and ill-paid service being a grant of Roman citizenship. Officered by Roman citizens, the lightly-armed auxiliaries were organized in a variety of ways, ranging from a lowly infantry cohort of 480 men to something as élite as an *ala milliaria*, consisting of 768 horsemen. It has been esti-mated that in Britain there were about ten auxiliary cohorts for every Roman legion, and there were four legions stationed in Britain during the 1st century A.D.

In 48 A.D. Scapula campaigned in North Wales, but had to retire due to trouble in the North of England. The following year he had to counter the cross-border raids of the Silures and, to stabilize the frontier near the Severn estuary, he ordered a legion (probably the *Twentieth Valereia Victrix*, originally from Cologne) to move from Colchester and establish itself at Gloucester. A second legion, or part of one (possibly the *Second Augusta*, originally from Strasbourg), may have been moved from Exeter to some unknown location on or near the Severn.

Preparations for an offensive were obviously in the making for legionaries to be stationed in strength so close to Silurian territory. Legionaries were the élite of the

Roman army—heavily armed, well-trained infantrymen, all of them Roman citizens. At full strength a legion numbered over 6,000 men, but its nominal strength may have been around 5,000. Apart from those who served as command personnel, the legionaries were organized into ten cohorts, nine of which comprised of 480 men at full strength, whereas the First Cohort (the most senior of them all) had ten centuries totalling 800 men. Legionaries were extremely loyal to their commanding officer, a legate, who was a nobleman of senatorial rank.

Using both legionaries and auxiliaries, Scapula attacked the Silures who had put their trust in Caratacus on account of his many battles, but Caratacus made a fatal mistake in c.51 A.D., engaging the Romans in pitched battle, albeit from a defensive position in the border area of North Wales, and had to flee only to be taken prisoner and escorted to Rome. The Silures, however, were far from finished and Tacitus provides a glimpse of the fighting that went on in South Wales, the result, he claimed, of a rumour that they were to be transported to Gaul. The trouble started when a detachment of legionaries under a camp prefect (a legion's second-in-command) was engaged in building a fort in Silurian territory, possibly at Clyro. The detachment was suddenly attacked, suffering the loss of the prefect, eight centurions and an unrecorded number of brave men before being rescued in the nick of time by auxiliaries from neighbouring forts. The situation worsened when a foraging party was put to flight, for this led to a battle, involving both legionaries and auxiliaries, for the situation to be brought under control—or so it seemed until two auxiliary cohorts marched into a trap, the survivors distributed as slaves throughout Wales.

Scapula died in 52 A.D., 'worn out with care'. By the time his successor, Didius Gallus, arrived on the scene a legion had suffered defeat and the Silures were running amok over a wide area. Didius managed to contain the Silures; he even advanced the frontier by building new forts in their territory. The details of this and subsequent campaigns are obscure and remain so for the next 22 years. It is left to the archaeologist to make sense of the vague statements made by Tacitus, but the evidence, such as it is, suggests that by the late '50s the main legionary base was at Usk, a fortress supported by an unknown number of auxiliary forts, plus what may have been *vexillation* forts (occupied by detachments of legionaries) at Clyro and Cardiff. Then, with the arrival of Britain's 10th governor, Julius Frontinus, in late 73 or early 74, the fog begins to clear a little, for we are told, in a sentence, that he overcame both the tenacity of the Silures and the physical difficulties of their land—and it is the nature of the terrain that enabled the Silures to give the Romans such a hard time.

Frontinus's Strategy

An able soldier and the author of several military treatises, Julius Frontinus was Governor of Britain for approximately four years. When he arrived to take up his appointment he found that the troublesome North of England had already been conquered by his predecessor, leaving him free to concentrate on subjugating the Silures. His commanders in the field would have left him in no doubt as to what they

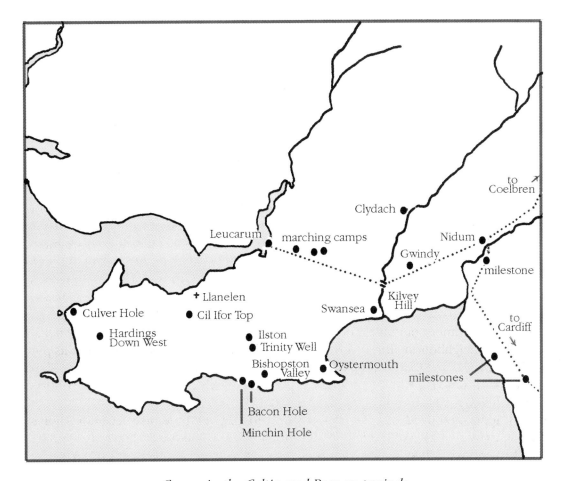

Gower in the Celtic and Roman periods.

were up against. They may have told him that the Silures painted themselves with blue woad (according to Caesar all the inhabitants of Britain did this), and may even have described them in much the same way as Tacitus described the opposition in an assault on Anglesey in 60 A.D.—'a fierce mass of warriors, the women like furies, black-robed with dishevelled hair, brandishing torches [into whose hands no Roman should fall] and the Druids, raising their hands to heaven and screaming terrible curses'. They were a people who would rarely be drawn into battle, but would fall upon Roman troops when they least expected it.

Unit commanders would certainly have told Frontinus that much of Silurian territory was mountainous, a vast forest, even on the coastal plains where low-lying marshlands added to the difficulties. Inland the valleys were impassable; in most cases the only way forward was to follow the ridgeways where the woodland was reported to be less dense. The terrain put Roman troops at a disadvantage, for they preferred to engage on open ground and in orderly formations so that their strict discipline and superior battle tactics would enable them to carry the day. In the depth of woods it was every man for himself.

If the forts and roadways that were established as a result of his campaigns are anything to go by, then it seems likely that Frontinus chose to make several seaborne landings, but there is no tangible evidence in the coastal lowlands to indicate actual troop movements. On the high ground between the valleys, however, there are the faint remains of Roman marching camps. Whenever legionaries were on campaign they each carried two wooden stakes. At the end of a day's march they dug a ditch to enclose their camp-site, placing the spoil to form a bank into which they embedded their stakes. Thus they had a measure of protection against surprise attacks. No such camps have been found in Gower, but on a ridgeway between the Swansea and Neath valleys the remains of a marching camp has been found at Coelbren, the banks enclosing an area of 35 acres, large enough to accommodate a legion and several auxiliary cohorts. The siting of this and other marching camps suggest that Frontinus executed a series of pincer movements from the coastal plains and from the Cardiff-Usk-Clyro line of forts.

Leucarum

As part of a long-term strategy the whole of Silurian territory was studded with auxiliary forts linked by a network of roads. Each fort was separated one from another by a day's march, and all were based on the new legionary fortress at Caerleon, the regimental headquarters of the *Second Augusta Legion* for the next 300 years. One auxiliary fort was sited at Neath (*Nidum*); another was situated at Loughor and, according to the 3rd century *Antonine Itinerary*, this fort was named *Leucarum*, from *Leuc*, the name of the river, meaning bright or shining water.

The actual location of *Leucarum* did not come to light until 1969, when an archaeologist discovered part of the fort wall and the foundations of an internal corner-turret in the side of the mound on which Loughor Castle stands. The turret proved to be the south-eastern corner of the fort which, shaped like a playing card, occupied the sloping ground between the castle and the Loughor estuary. It is believed that *Leucarum* occupied an area of approximately five acres, large enough to accommodate a mixed cohort of auxiliary infantry and cavalry (*cohors quingenaria equitata*) which, at full strength, would have numbered 608 men under the command of a prefect (*praefecti cohors*) who was a Roman citizen.

The prefect of a mixed cohort had at his disposal six infantry centuries of 80 men, each commanded by a *centurion* who was supported by his second-in-command, an *optio*, a standard-bearer who held the title of *signifer*, and a clerk known as a *tesserius*. The prefect also had under his command 128 horsemen, organized into four troops of 32 men, each troop led by a *decurion*. At the time of Claudius's invasion (43 A.D.), the men serving in auxiliary cohorts are likely to have come from the Balkans, Gaul, the Low Countries and Spain, but by the time of Frontinus's governorship these cohorts had been in Britain for thirty years and we can be fairly certain that the auxiliaries of Frontinus's day were either the sons of former auxiliaries, or they had been recruited from within the Roman province of Britain.

When the auxiliaries arrived at *Leucarum* about 75 A.D. they constructed a fort which they surrounded with a ditch backed up by a huge earthen rampart. The rampart was contained by a massive, outward-facing palisade, perhaps 5m. high, behind which the rampart sloped inwards over a distance of about 6m. Many years later, probably during the reign of Trajan (98 - 117 A.D.), the palisade was replaced by a metre-thick stone wall. Then, about 130 A.D., the internal area was reduced by the construction of another wall which cut off the south-western half of the fort, suggesting a reduction in the size of the garrison. *Leucarum* may have

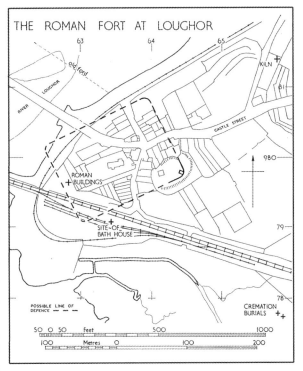

The Roman fort at Loughor.
(Crown copyright RCHAMW)

been abandoned altogether shortly after the last-mentioned date. Coins and cooking pots and the recutting of ditches suggest that the fort may have been reoccupied in the late 3rd century as part of a coastal defense system against Irish raiders, whose attacks began in the 3rd century and reached a climax in the 4th.

It can be assumed that a large part of the fort's interior was occupied by barrack blocks which would have several times undergone reconstruction due to the climate, for Tacitus describes British weather as unpleasantly wet, with rain and mist frequent, but without extremes of cold. There is evidence to suggest that the fort may also have been subject to flooding, and the fact that the south-western corner now lies beneath water at high tide may have occasioned the abandonment of that part of the fort.

The layout of barrack blocks and various buildings within the fort would have adhered to a set plan, the central area being occupied by the headquarters building (*principia*), one room of which contained the regimental shrine. A pagan altar that may have stood in this holy of holies is in the Swansea Museum; it serves as a reminder that Roman troops took their religious beliefs and cult practices seriously. A great many artefacts have been found at Loughor over the last 150 years—pottery, numerous coins, objects made of glass, tiles, querns, weapons and, surprisingly, even plate armour. A few miles to the west are the remains of three practice camps where auxiliaries, as part of their training, constructed small marching camps, paying particular attention to the entrances.

Life at *Leucarum* could not have been entirely without comfort, for a bath-house was discovered in 1851 during construction of the now defunct railway station. It is more than probable that, despite official policy, soldiers married local girls, their sons raised to become soldiers once they were old enough. After 25 years service soldiers are likely to have set up a business on the road leading eastwards, offering anything that might be required by their still serving comrades.

Roads

Roman roads were not dirt tracks, but raised roadways as much as 6m. wide and 2m .high, the upper surface paved, with stone kerbs in place. Roads such as these were astonishing feats of engineering, for not only did they run straight for many miles— uphill and down dale, through woods and marshland—but their construction involved a great deal of labour—slave labour perhaps—because, apart from the accu-mulation of huge amounts of earth and stone, a great many trees had to be cut down on either side of the roadways to reduce the risk of ambush.

No Roman roads have survived locally, but we have a fair idea where a road, such as we have described, traversed the land between the Loughor and Tawe rivers. Imagine a century of auxiliary foot soldiers passing out through the gateway of *Leucarum*, the men following their mounted centurion, their *signifer* marching ahead with the century standard held aloof for all to see. If these auxiliaries had marched out of *Leucarum*, heading for the fort at Neath, they would have probably marched in a straight line over much the same route as the modern A4070—over Garn Goch Common as far the Ivorites Public House at Fforestfach, then up over Middle Road to Grid Reference 632 660, where the straight line of modern roadway ends. If the auxiliaries pressed on, more or less in a straight line towards the Tawe River, they would have arrived at Grid Reference 661 945 where, in the 19th century, a ford was discovered, made of oak beams that were rebated together.

Beyond the ford there are no clues as to the line of march taken by the auxil-iaries, although it is possible that they passed the standing stone at Bon-y-maen. Apart from the remains of two stone gateways (both of them fenced off with iron rail-ings) there is nothing to be seen of *Nidum* (Neath) above ground, but Banana Island, on the main road between Neath Abbey and Cadoxton, lies within the area occupied by the southern half of the fort. The auxiliaries, having reached this fort, would have travelled 12 English miles. Had they gone west, fording the Loughor estuary by an old ford which, at one time, could only be used during intervals of four hours between tides, they would have been on the road to the auxiliary fort of *Moridunum*, now buried under Carmarthen town.

The Aftermath of War

Frontinus, having defeated the Silures, does not appear to have dealt harshly with them, although it is quite likely that many of their young men would have been drafted into the Roman army to become, perhaps, one of a dozen British cohorts that are known to have served in the Army of the Danube. There is no evidence to support the idea that Silurian hill-forts were systematically destroyed. Roman pottery found in five Gower hill-forts is evidence that the locals continued to live in defended settlements even in the 2nd century A.D. Indeed, a shard of mid-2nd century Samian ware was actually found beneath the ramparts of a hill-fort on Kilvey Hill, proving that the fort had been built long after the Roman conquest.

One fort that continued in use during Roman times overlooks Bishopston Valley. This is a promontory fort, occupying a steep-sided ridge within a loop of a small river, the interior measuring less than 1¼ acres. To the west, the neck of the ridge is traversed by two close-set banks and ditches. When excavated, the site of a hut was marked by a hearth and five post-holes set in an oval. Finds included a brooch of Roman date, an iron finger-ring, slingstones, a shard of what may have been Iron Age B pottery and a piece of Samian ware of 1st to 2nd century date. The bones of ox, pig, sheep and red deer were also unearthed, as well as a variety of sea shells. All things considered, the occupants of this fort do not appear to have been prosperous.

A total of five caves have yielded material—namely pottery and coins—that can be assigned to the Roman period. Two of these caves were probably used for burial. The remaining three are believed to have been inhabited, but only Minchin Hole in the cliffs south of Pennard is worthy of mention, if only because of its sheer size. The entrance alone is 10m. high by 5m. wide, whereas the interior extends some 50m. into the cliffs, at the same time widening to over 20m. Among the objects found were Iron Age B and Belgic pottery, metalwork and fragments of 1st to 2nd century Roman ware.

Benefits for Some

Roman rule brought peace, an end to internecine warfare, and gradually, as the scars of war healed, the leaders of Silurian society, the men who held power and wealth, were encouraged to adopt a romanized way of life. To become ideal Roman citizens they were persuaded to wear the toga, to build town houses, to take part in local self-government, and so, in the space of a generation or more, *Venta Silurum* (Caerwent), the capital of the *Respublica Civitatus Silurum* came into existence. In other words the leading men became members of an *ordo* (a council) which managed the affairs of the *Civitas* of the Silures. Of course, it cannot be said with certainty that all the leading men were Silures. There is evidence to suggest that it was Roman policy to lump together a number of tribes to create a *civitas* and assign to it the name of the most prominent tribe.

The Silures living in the fertile plains of Monmouthshire and Glamorgan were to benefit from their proximity to the already romanized regions of southern Britain. In the 2nd century A.D. villas begin to appear in the easterly parts of Silurian territory, a sign of a thriving economy. Further west, in remote places such as Gower, the material benefits in the lowland areas appear to have been little more than Roman pottery and coins—for example, there seems to have been some sort of settlement in the Castle Street/Wind Street area of Swansea City because J.G. Rutter, in his *Pre-historic Gower* (published 1949), records that fragments of a Roman cooking pot and early 4th century coins have been found in the area.

That said, there appears to have been a villa at Oystermouth because Rutter records that fragments of a mosaic pavement were found in the churchyard of All Saints Church, and these, along with shards of Roman pottery and coins, point to something far more substantial than a hut. Anyone who could afford a mosaic pavement must have worn the toga, spoken Latin as a first or second language and been driven round in a wicker chariot. Most probably the man would have been a romanized Celt, waited upon by slaves and living off the labours of his bond tenants whose work would have been regulated by a churlish bailiff, wielding a stick.

The one place in Gower that appears to have been unaffected by the conquest is the uplands north of the present M4 Motorway. The deteriorating climate of the Bronze Age is believed to have worsened in the Iron Age, the increased rainfall combining with a colder climate to render upland soil fit for nothing more than the cultivation of oats, a cereal that first made its appearance in Britain in the Late Bronze Age. The upland population must surely have been sparse—only two hill-forts out of the 37 referred to above are to be found in this mountainous hinterland; there are no Roman artefacts here, for this is where tribesmen carried on as they had done for centuries, keeping alive a way of life that would, one day, enable the Celts to return to their past.

The paucity of well-to-do settlement sites gives the impression that, by and large, the natives of Gower did not benefit materially from over 300 years of Roman rule. Yet it is obvious from the evidence of coin hoards that certain locals had accumulated wealth in the form of Roman currency. The largest hoard recorded by Rutter amounts to about 500 coins, dated to between 260 and 273, discovered at Gwindy, Llansamlet. Two smaller hoards were found at Ilston, one of about 200 coins dated 54 to 180, and another, found with a skeleton, consisted of 91 coins dated 260 to 282. The dating of most hoards coincides with the attacks of Irish raiders which began in the region of the Severn Estuary about the middle of the 3rd century and reached a climax when barbarians from Ireland, northern Scotland and the Continent made a concerted attack on Britain and northern Europe in 367. Milestones in the Port Talbot area point to road improvements, probably by the military, between 238 and 324, presumably to facilitate troops movements, and the fort of *Leucarum* seems to have been reoccupied for coastal defence towards the end of the 3rd century.

Judging by the coin evidence, the villas in south-east Wales had ceased to exist by the middle of the 4th century, whereas in southern England the coin evidence suggests that they continued in use until at least the end of the century. There is, however, a problem with coin evidence in that the number of 4th century coins that were shipped to Britain decreased whenever Roman troops were withdrawn for service elsewhere. The coin shipments would have ceased altogether during the occasions between 383 and 411 when troops stationed in Britain elected men to be emperors in opposition to the legitimate emperors of Rome.

A Change in Belief

In his *De Bello Gallico* Julius Caesar wrote:

> Druids officiate at religious gatherings; they give rulings on all religious questions. Young men flock to them in large numbers for instruction, for they are held in great honour by their people. They assume the role of judges in almost all disputes, between tribes and individuals. When a crime is committed, or a dispute arises over inheritance or boundaries, it is they who adjudicate and calculate the compensation to be paid and received. Any individual or tribe which fails to accept their awards is banned from taking part in any sacrifice - the worst punishment to be meted out on any individual or tribe, for they are regarded as criminals, shunned by all.

Caesar also claimed that the Druidic doctrine originated in Britain, that those who wished to study it went there for instruction, but there is nothing to support a Druidic presence in Britain other than Tacitus's report that, in 60 A.D., when the governor, Suetonius Paulinus, lined his troops up on the south side of the Menia Straights he saw, on the Anglesey shore, 'Druids raising their hands to heaven and screaming terrible curses'. When the island was taken, Suetonius ordered that the oak groves dedicated to barbarous superstitions be destroyed.

When the influence that the Druids had over their fellow-countrymen is considered, one may wonder why it is the Celts abandoned their old belief to embrace Christianity. It is not as if the Celts were incapable of holding onto their pagan belief. The Romans would not tolerate their priests, the Druids. Yet in Britain there are hints that Druidism survived Roman rule; moreover, the Romans paralleled their gods with those of the Celts, presumably in an attempt to merge one with the other, the native deities being the losers. Yet in Wales the native deities survived the Roman period.

In Ireland the transition from paganism to Christianity was almost a merger, and for good reason—there were similarities in the two beliefs. The priesthood of both religions taught that there was life after death, the older order teaching reincarnation, the new preaching the Resurrection; the one held oak trees to be sacred, the other looked to the Cross. Of course, the Celts had numerous gods and goddesses, many of them linked to regions or tribes, but one of their gods appear to have been a father-like figure—in Irish mythology he is *Daghda*. Connected to the father figure is the mother-earth-goddess associated with fertility and, later, in Ireland in particular, she is associated with the Virgin Mary. Interestingly, at Culver Hole in Gower a bronze figurine has been found, its form that of a nursing mother-earth-goddess.

The older order had its equivalent of a human figure of divine birth who died in his prime. The Irish called him *Lugh the Shining One* and his name is perpetuated in place-names such as Lyons in France. In the course of conversion, the saints replaced deities and warrior-heroes, the saints displaying a moral courage that enabled them to stand up to kings. Saints are often associated with particular localities and when they died they were revered in such a way that they became cult figures, to whom later writers accredited with supernatural powers.

Early Christians attached a special significance to water in that they baptized converts by total immersion. The pagan Celts saw watery places, particularly springs and pools, as the doorways between their world and the world of their gods. Whenever they sought favours from their gods they placed their votive offerings in watery places; hence the bronze and iron objects found at Llyn Fawr. Perhaps the story of King Arthur's sword being thrown into a lake is an echo of the practice, and holy wells, of which Gower has several, may point to a survival of contacting the Divine through water. Trinity Well in the Ilston Valley is not only the best-known holy well in Gower, but its connection with St. Cenydd suggests that it was old enough for it to have been revered as a holy place by both pagans and Christians.

The Early Christian Communities

Christianity had more to offer than the belief and barbaric practices of the Druids. Yet the evangelizing movement got off to a slow start. Archaeology has provided evidence to suggest there had been an early Christian community in the Silurian capital at Caerwent. It had been the norm for such communities to be centred on a town, but a new format was about to change all that, for early in the 4th century thousands of Egyptian Christians had chosen to live in isolated communities in the desert, away from the stresses and distractions of the secular world. Then, later in the century, St. Martin of Tours encouraged the practice of Christians living in isolated communities in the west so that by their example others might seek a better life. From Gaul this new practice—monasticism—arrived in Britain via the Severn Estuary and seems to have taken root in what is now southern Herefordshire. Unfortunately, what little is known of the movement is cloaked in legend.

For example, in 383, Magnus Maximus, a high-ranking army officer, took troops out of Britain and made himself Emperor of Britain, Gaul and Spain, but was killed by a legitimate emperor in 388. According to tradition, Magnus had married Elen, a native of North Wales, and while in Gaul both Magnus and Elen came into contact with St. Martin. After Magnus's death, Elen returned to Britain, so the story goes, and brought with her St. Martin's views on monasticism. It would appear that she settled in southern Herefordshire, for that is where we find a monastery dedicated to her; from there her followers may have travelled westwards, one group settling in north Gower to found a cell—a small religious house dependent on a larger one—dedicated to Elen.

Of course, it cannot be said with certainty that the place-name Llanelen is linked to the Elen mentioned above, for the only reference to Llanelen as an ecclesiastical site comes from Isaac Hamon who, writing in the late 17th century, claimed there had been three chapels in the parish of Llanrhidian, one of them Llanelen, although Hamon referred to it as Wernhalog, the name of a nearby farm. A total of 31 graves support the view that there had been an early church here, while excavation has revealed seven post holes which may represent a small, timber church, later replaced by a two-chambered, stone building, undoubtedly a church, the western chamber of which, the nave, measured 6m. by 4m. and had a doorway in the west wall. A small chancel was later attached to the east wall of the nave. Historical records relating to the early 13th century make no mention of Llanelen, suggesting that the church had become defunct by then. Nowadays Llanelen is the name of a nearby farm.

Raiders Turned Settlers

Following their concerted attack on the romanized part of Britain in 367, the barbarians continued to harry the country on all sides: the *Picti* of the Scottish Highlands several times overran Hadrian's Wall, Germanic sea rovers menaced the coastline from the North Sea and the English Channel; in the west the Irish—who were never conquered by the Romans—turned from raiding to colonizing the most westerly parts of Britain—the Western Isles, Kintyre, the Isle of Man, Anglesey, the Llyn Peninsula, West Wales and the West Country; they also appear to have had a presence in Gower— reason for us to consider an unexplained linguistic difference among the Celts.

The P and Q Branches of the Celtic Language

When Classical writers turned their attention to southern Britain they referred to the inhabitants by a variety of names such as *Pretani* and later *Britanni*; they were the people who, prior to the arrival of Angles and Saxons, occupied all Britain south of the Scottish Highlands. It has already been said that the language of the Gauls and that of the *Britanni* were closely related, but further west the Irish spoke a Celtic language that was noticeably different. Philologists—people who study languages—refer to the Gaelic of Ireland as Q Celtic to distinguish it from the P Celtic language of the *Britanni* and the Gauls. One of the most striking differences between these two branches of the Celtic language is the Gaelic use of a K sound which, in the language of the *Britanni*, comes across as a P sound—for example, the *Britanni* at one time called themselves the *Pretani*, whereas the Irish called them the *Cruithne*.

Several sources record that a branch of the *Uí Liatháin*, a *clanna* that held sway over a territory near Cork in southern Ireland, established itself in West Wales and may, therefore, have been largely responsible for encouraging Irish settlement in the land of the Demetae, especially in the pre-1974 counties of Pembrokeshire and Cardiganshire where numerous place-names point to a strong Irish presence. The same counties contain more than 20 ogham-inscribed memorial stones—ogham being an ancient Irish alphabet of 20 characters formed by parallel strokes on either side of a continuous line as, for example, the edge of a roughly-hewn, rectangular-stone. Isolated examples of these stones can be found all over Wales and, in his *Historia Brittonum*, a Celtic scribe known to historians as Nennius stated that the *Uí*

Liatháin obtained the Land of the Demetae, and also the provinces of Cydweli and Gower until they were driven out by Cunedda and his sons, implying that the *Uí Líatháin* claimed overlordship over a wide area which included Cydweli and Gower.

Of course, migrations across the Irish Sea were not all one way. There are references in Irish literature to ruling *Cruithne* communities on the island, several of them bearing the names of tribes known to have originated in Britain. The migratory character of the Celts is apparent within Britain as well. One migration, involving part of a northern border tribe known as the Votadini (who were responsible for holding the northern frontier beyond Hadrain's Wall), took place in the late 4th or early 5th century. The leaders of this migration were Cunedda and his sons; they are said to have expelled the Irish from North Wales with great slaughter, and also driven the *Uí Liatháin* out of Cydweli and Gower.

There are, however, many who would question the historicity of Cunedda, partly because what little is known of him was written in the early 9th century—more than 400 years after his alleged migration. Be that as it may, the Irish undoubtedly had a presence in Gower, for there are two place-names—Clydach and Cnoc Coch, Llansamlet—which, in part, are borrowings from Gaelic; moreover, there is an ogham inscription, dated to the 5th or early 6th century, on the Roman altar found at *Leucarum*, the only word that is distinguishable being *Lica*, which means stone.

A Return to the Past

Except for tribes such as the Votadini, 300 years of Roman rule had robbed the *Britanni* of the will to fight. Under the *Pax Romana* they had come to rely on an army to protect them. All that was fine until the Roman Empire began to fall apart, its frontiers overrun by barbarians, its army wasted by civil wars. What troops were available were needed to protect Rome, not far-off Britain. For a while the *Britanni* managed to stem the tide of invasion by hiring mercenaries, or by relocating tribes such as the Votadini, but it was only a matter of time before the *Britanni* were forced to fend for themselves, and to do that they had to return to their heroic past. That is not to say they became barbarians, for Roman law still prevailed among the more romanized *Britanni*, but those in the west and in the north became so warlike that they were able to hold their own for centuries, the result being that in places such as Gower a modified Celtic Culture developed in isolation.

Chapter III
The Indigenous Welsh

The End of Roman *Britanniae*

In response to a plea for help the Roman emperor, Honorius, issued a letter in or about 410, instructing the *Britanni* to see to their own defence. This was easier said than done because *Britanniae* had no standing army. What it inherited was the late Roman practice of giving land to barbarians in return for military service. From Kent to Northumberland, Germanic mercenaries were stationed near the coast and, for 15 years, they appear to have been successful in keeping undesirables out. Unfortunately, they encouraged more of their own people in. Their numbers increased. In or about 442 they revolted and the fighting raged, albeit intermittently, until, in the last quarter of the 5th century, the *Britanni* raised an outstanding leader.

King Arthur—a Shadowy Figure Clothed in Legend

One theory concerning Arthur is that he was the warlord of Elmet, a small kingdom in the vicinity of Leeds and, that after inflicting several defeats on the Germanic settlers east of the River Trent he was accepted by the *Britanni* as their 'Leader of Battles'. Arthur went on to defeat the foreigners on several fronts, forcing them to agree to what the Celtic monk, Gildas, called the 'melancholy partition of Britanniae with the barbarians', which kept them within certain bounds. There are strong hints in Welsh tradition that Arthur was a tyrant who raised numerous warbands to force even his own people to bend to his will. His government may have been in office when Gildas referred to a time in his youth when the restraints of truth and justice were still observed when rulers, persons both public and private, bishops and clergy, all kept their station. Arthur would appear to have passed through Gower, for on the windswept heights of Cefn Bryn the megalithic tomb known as Arthur's Stone has a legend attached to it that says Arthur removed the stone from his shoe whilst at Llanelli and threw it so that it landed on Cefn Bryn.

Gower in the Dark Ages

The period between 410 and the Anglo-Norman Conquest (the early 12th century in the case of Gower) is referred to as the Early Middle Ages, better known as the Dark Ages—dark not because it was necessarily barbaric, but because our knowledge of those 700 years is fragmented, the historicity of the material open to question. In the 5th century, Gower was still a wild, inhospitable place, a land cloaked in forest, abounding in extensive bogs, except perhaps in the more fertile parts of the Peninsula, although even there valleys such as Clyne and the one below Penrice were, no doubt, still thickly wooded. The climate at that time was in decline—an increase in rainfall, floods and great frosts all conspired to make life difficult. Crop failure followed by famine would have been a frequent occurrence and the situation probably persisted until, in the 11th century, the climate improved, becoming similar to what it is today.

Whether on horseback or on foot, travelling in Gower would have been a hazardous undertaking with no signs to point the way, no bridges across rivers and streams, and in the uplands there was always a chance, prior to the 6th century, of coming face to face with a brown bear. How long the Roman road through Gower

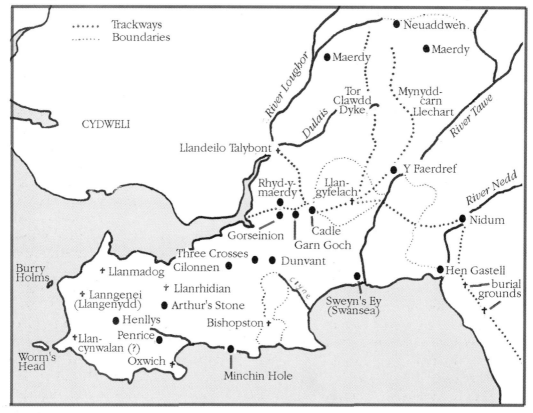

Gower in the Dark Ages.

remained in use is unknown, but by the 8th century an alternative route from the ruins of *Nidum* may have passed Llansamlet Church, crossed the Tawe above Morriston and brought weary, wet-legged travellers to the monastery of Llangyfelach; from there two trackways led northwards—one over Mynydd Carnllechart (which may have been established in the Bronze Age), the other led to Penlle'r Castell, passing Tor Clawdd where, at Grid Reference 669 065 (approximately), there is a dyke, constructed probably in the 8th century to bar the way of cattle raiders and the like. The main coastal highway, however, continued westwards to Penllergaer where it forked, the right fork leading to the ford at Pontardulais, the left to the treacherous tidal waters of the Loughor estuary.

Early Christian Communities

In the 5th century monasticism gained ground in south-east Wales, aided perhaps by refugees from war-torn regions where barbarian attacks and civil strife were destroying the peace and prosperity of the Roman world, a consequence of which was that more and more people sought refuge in the Christian faith, detaching themselves from a chaotic world by living in monastic communities. One such community was that of Llanilltud Fawr in the Vale of Glamorgan, otherwise known as Llantwit Major. Its founder, St. Illtud, who flourished in the late 5th to early 6th century, has numerous dedications between Kidwelly and Cardiff. At one time it was believed that churches dedicated to him were founded by him or his disciples whereas, nowadays, historians accept that many dedications to Illtud (and to other saints as well) came into existence long after the saint's death, the consequence of a cult wishing to perpetuate his name.

St. Illtud has three dedications in Gower—the parish churches of Ilston, Oxwich and Llanrhidian. Yet none of these churches have a history prior to the 12th century. Only the church at Llanrhidian can claim an ancient past, and that rests partly on the fact that an early 6th-century stone monument, now lost, was reported to have stood a little to the west of the present-day parish church. In the 16th century someone sketched the monument which bore an inscription in mainly Roman capitals that is difficult to decipher. Another inscribed stone, in the porch of the present-day church, which probably served as a lintel, has two human or angelic figures carved into its surface and is dated to the 9th or 10th century. The two stones on the green outside the church are of unknown origin.

Memorial stones with inscriptions in Roman capitals are usually found in isolation. Obviously the one at Llanrhidian once marked the burial place of a well-to-do or well-known person, even a saint, and could easily have become a focus for devotion and later burials, which puts in mind the place-name *merthyr*, meaning martyr, and points to a practice common in Wales whereby a burial, or burials, preceded a church. This may have been the origin of Llanrhidian, though why the church should be dedicated to two saints (St. Illtud and St. Rhidian) is a mystery. It may be that, originally, the church had been dedicated to Rhidian and that, at a later date, it was rededicated to Illtud. Whatever the truth, all three Illtud dedications were probably subject to the

abbots of Llanilltud Fawr; that is, until the 12th century when the monastery's importance was eclipsed by Anglo-Norman conquerors.

Early Christian graveyards are identified by the fact that the dead were buried
with their feet to the east, heads to the west, the belief being that when they rose from
the dead they would face east, in the direction of the Holy Land. They were interred
without grave good which makes them difficult to date and ascribe to any particular
culture. Only three early Christian graveyards have been found in Gower—one at
Llanelen, one on the Island of Burry Holms and a third which occupied the same piece
of ground as the present-day ruins of Swansea Castle. The first two are undoubtedly
Celtic because they were both sited close to a Celtic church, whereas the Swansea
Castle site was in an Anglo-Norman town, the nearest church being 150m. away

Occasionally, caves may also have been used for burials as seems to have been the
case at Culver Hole, Llangenydd, and at Bacon Hole, Pennard, where one or two Dark
Age artifacts have been found. Minchin Hole, Pennard, is another possibility, although
here three hearth areas and several finds suggest intermittent domestic occupation
during the first five centuries A.D.

Kings and Tyrants

In his *De Excidio Conquesta Britanniae* (The Ruin and Conquest of Britain), written
in the early 530s, Gildas speaks of public offices which 'he claimed' still existed in
Britanniae 120 years after its split with Rome. He also refers to high-ranking military
commanders called *duces*, denouncing them as tyrannical kings who, with their
warbands, intimidated public officials and caused civil wars. What this meant is that
the *Britanni* were returning to their Celtic past, becoming the subjects of many dynasties, often warring among themselves.

The Kingdom of Gower

The *Civitas* of the Silures did not survive as an entity, but fragmented into several
petty kingdoms. References to this political fragmentation abound in a group of
manuscripts known as the *Lives*, each manuscript a colourful biography of an important, usually 6th-century saint, and it is from the *Lives* we learn that, about 500, one
Glywys conquered much that had once been Silurian territory, Gower included, and
that on his death, when his kingdom was divided between his heirs, his son,
Merchwyn, had Gower as his portion. Unfortunately, the *Lives* cannot be relied upon
as history—most of them were written in the late 11th or early 12th century to empha-
size the importance of saints whose names were linked to existing churches, monasteries and holy wells by presenting the saints as the sons of important men, even
kings, and by crediting them with supernatural powers.

There is, however, one manuscript that is considered more reliable than the
Lives, and that is the *Liber Landavensis*—the Llandaff Charters—which was written
in the early 12th century by a scribe who claimed that the charters had been copied
from a much older book called the *Llyfr Teilo*, which no longer exists. These ancient

charters confirm that, by the early 6th century, south-east Wales had become politically fragmented, that Gower was indeed an independent kingdom; moreover, one charter confirms the existence of King Merchwyn ap Glywys, for his name appears among the witnesses to a grant of land in Gower to Dubricius, Archbishop of Llandaff. This particular grant is important in that it is the earliest reliable reference there is of Gower.

Merchwyn may have lived in a hill-fort such as Hen Gastell, situated near the western end of what is now the M4 Briton Ferry bypass. This particular hill-fort was a high-status settlement occupied in the 5th and 6th centuries. Recent excavation at the site unearthed pottery remains from as far afield as Greece and Asia Minor—pottery that would have contained wine and oil. Other finds included a great deal of coloured glass, the remains of drinking vessels. About 1,000 animal bones were retrieved from the ditch, the majority of which came from cows and pigs; there were also the remains of a few sheep, goats and horses.

In line with other petty kings, Merchwyn maintained his position with the aid of a warband that was bonded to him by an exchange of gifts: he provided food and drink, shared spoil and granted land; in return his warrior-companions agreed to support him, enabling him to sway over the surrounding peasantry, to accompany him wherever he went. He himself travelled and fought on horseback, as did his principal companions, but the bulk of his retinue were youths, the sons of privileged free men, commended to wait upon him and to serve as lightly-armed foot soldiers.

Privileged Free Men
Merchwyn did not wield power for his own benefit, but did so as much for the benefit and security of the privileged free men with whom he shared power and wealth. As to who the privileged men were, the answer can, in part, be found in the charter he witnessed, which records that Gwordog gave his daughter, Dulon, to the Archbishop of Llandaff to be a nun and also gave 26 acres of land to the Archbishop in perpetual consecration. Apart from King Merchwyn the charter was witnessed by Madawy, Garw, Llgwy and Lunaed, most of whom—if not all—were local landowners; along with Gwordog they were the privileged free men known as the *uchelwyr*, the high/best/better men who were the heads of households, the upholders of public opinion, the enforcers of tribal law. Such men were the companions and advisors of their king, accompanying him on warlike expeditions, commending their sons to serve in his retinue. The more influential of the *uchelwyr* imitated Merchwyn in that not only did they travel and fight on horseback, but they had small retinues of their own. They were men not to be scorned, for there were occasions when kings were dispatched by their privileged subjects.

Below the *uchelwyr* were sons (and grandsons) known as *bonheddigion*, each of whom might be settled on their father's land, but only after the death of their fathers did they ascend to the status of *uchelwyr*, the whole of their fathers land and moveable property being, then, divided equally between them, irrespective of whether they were half-brothers, legitimate or not, a practice known as gavelkind. In cases where one son died before the father, then grandsons had a claim to what would have been their dead father's share in the inheritance. According to Gerald of Wales, gavelkind led to lawsuits, quarrels, murders, feuds and, it may be added, mindless warfare. The practice undoubtedly contributed to the downfall of the *Britanni* because their kingdoms were often divided between sons on the death of a king, thereby limiting their capacity to wage war. With regards to the *uchelwyr*, gavelkind led to estates becoming progressively smaller so that, by the 16th century, the descendants of most free men were little more than yeoman farmers.

Dominant though they were, the free men were not the most numerous class. According to the *Domesday Survey* of 1086-7—which records the ownership of land in England and several border areas in Wales—31% of the native population were free men. In the 6th century the proportion is likely to have been much smaller.

Halls and House-platforms

The principal building at Merchwyn's court would have been the hall, a timber-built longhouse with a huge ridge roof of straw, the eaves almost touching the ground. The law tracts that have survived from the 13th century onwards describe the hall of a king as of two parts, separated by a central fire. Both parts were occupied mainly by long tables and it would, therefore, be easy to imagine Merchwyn and the male members of his household carousing, laughing, banging on the tables, the flickering light of the fire reflecting off their half-shadowed faces. While dogs snarled and fought over the cast-off food that had been tossed to the straw-covered floor, all eyes may have been on an itinerant bard, moving around the tables, dramatizing his words with gestures.

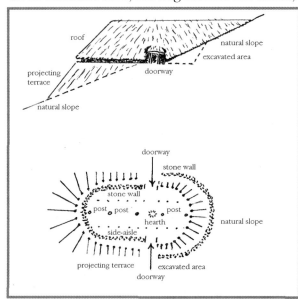

Later, when the revelry was at an end, the men retired to the low-roofed side-aisles that served as sleeping quarters.

Sites that were occupied by the halls of free men are fairly numerous on the high ground between the Loughor and Tawe valleys, especially on the hills flanking the Dulais Valley. They are known to archaeologists as Medieval house-platforms, and are usually found on ridges where the ground curves before falling to steep-sided valleys. At each site a shelf had been dug into the hillside and the spoil deposited so as to form a projecting terrace. The

Medieval House-platform.

average platform is about 14m. by 7.5m.—the long axis at right angles to the slope—and excavations at similar sites in mid-Glamorgan make it plain that the levelled area was occupied by a longhouse.

An excavated site might yield a row of central post-holes, the posts originally supporting a ridge roof of thatch or turf. Low walls of turf or stone at the terrace end suggest that the roof-rafters must have rested upon them and carried the eaves almost to the ground. At the shelf end the roof appears to have covered the excavated area, the rafters resting upon the surrounding bank. Access to the interior would have been gained by either of two opposing doorways, each set in the long axis of the building at points level with the natural slope; the doorways were probably sheltered by porches. Inside, two rows of smaller post-holes mark the positions of supports for the rafters (between the ridge and the low walls of turf or stone), and also point to the existence of side-aisles for storage where the roof was low. Some sites have yielded evidence of external drainage ditches, central hearths, stone paving, flints and iron nails, fragments of Medieval cooking-pots (some of late 13th to early 14th century date) and iron slag, showing that a limited amount of metal had been worked on at least some of the sites.

The inference is that these house-platforms are the remains of all-year-round homesteads and that the occupants were engaged in cattle rearing, which they kept in the terrace end of their halls. About half the sites stand alone, a quarter are to be found in pairs, the remainder in groups of three or four. Except where potsherds have been found, no house-platform can be assigned to any particular period, but long-houses of this type were still in use during the Early Modern Period (after 1500).

In the Peninsula, where there was no requirement to dig into a hillside, the remains of a longhouse, measuring 14m. by 9m., have been found at Henllys—meaning Old Court—in the parish of Llandewi. The faint remains are on level ground within the north-eastern angle of an enclosure measuring 26m. by 23m.

In a Medieval tale called the *Dream of Rhonabwy* we have a glimpse of the conditions in which some people lived when travellers arrived at the hall of Heilyn Goch.

> As they [the travellers] approached the homestead of Heilyn Goch ap Cadwgan they could see an old hall, black with gable-ends, from which issued a great deal of smoke [through a hole in the roof]. On entering they found the floor uneven and full of puddles. Where there were bumps it was difficult to stand so slippery were they with the mire of cattle; where there were puddles a man might sink to his ankles in ooze. There were branches of holly spread over the floor, the cattle having browsed the sprigs. On the bare, dusty boards of one dais sat a crone, throwing husks into the fire, the ensuing smoke proving unbearable. On another dais was a yellow, calf skin upon which it would have been a blessing to sit.

Links to the South

Gower had strong links with the South West, especially Cornwall, Devon and part of Somerset which the Romans designated the *Civitas* of the Dumnonii, later to become known as Dumnonia. Ties existed with Brittany as well, which, in the early 5th century, had been wasted to the extent that even in the 6th century many villas still lay abandoned and overgrown—it was a country crying out for re-settlement. Migrants from *Britanniae* began arriving in Brittany soon after the German revolt of 442. A second migration began almost a hundred years later, the migrants coming mainly from the South West and from south-east Wales where a series of natural disasters caused the *Britanni* to flee these regions. The migration continued as a result of southern England falling into enemy hands, becoming so prolonged that north-western Gaul became known as *Lesser Britanniae* and is the reason why Brittany survived as a Celtic land, its people speaking a language that resembles Welsh. What these migrations have to do with Gower becomes clear when Hen Gastell and its trade links with the Mediterranean are considered.

The Plague

Natural disasters may, in part, have been responsible for the Germanic conquest of what we now know to be England. In 535 a volcanic eruption in the Far East sent so much ash into the atmosphere that it created a nuclear winter, lasting 18 months, an event confirmed by tree-rings and ice-core data. Throughout the world the temperature dropped; with insufficient sunlight, less water evaporated and a reduction in rainfall led to draught, crop failure, famine and to *Brittaniae* becoming a wasteland; worse, the bubonic plague, the result of climatic changes in Africa, hit Constantinople in 542 and spread like wildfire throughout the Mediterranean world. It swept through southern France and, from the Bay of Biscay, ships carried flea-infested rats to both Ireland and *Britanniae*, and to the Severn Estuary in particular, which in 547 was the main trading area of the *Britanni*. The bubonic plague depopulated the *Britanni*, and with so many corpses lying about the yellow plague—cholera—reared its ugly head, forcing many to flee to Brittany, which seems to have been spared the worse horrors.

The only reference to a natural disaster taking place in Gower in the 6th century comes from one of the Llandaff charters, which concerns the estate of Cingualan (which probably centred on Rhosili) 'which St. Oudoceus, Bishop of Llandaff, lost from the time of the mortality; that is, the yellow plague'. St. Oudocius had fled to Brittany to escape the plague; on his return he discovered that the followers of St. Illtud had laid claim to the Cingualan estate.

The Second Germanic Rebellion

There is reason to believe that the Germanic settlers in Sussex, Kent, East Anglia, Lincolnshire and Leicestershire, south Yorkshire and Northumberland escaped the worst effects of both plagues; they traded with northern Europe, not the Mediterranean, and the *Britanni* would have nothing to do with them. It was only a matter of time before the Germanic people realized there was a population vacuum beyond their borders. Yet the evidence points to a situation in which the more affluent *Britanni* of southern England were still employing German mercenaries to

Britain in the Dark Ages.

guard their borders. It appears that these later mercenaries were the ones who initiated the second Germanic revolt, for in 571 they turned on the *Britanni* of the east Midlands, routing them near Bedford, and from that moment on the Germanic people were everywhere on the move. In 577 the *Britanni* were so decisively defeated at the Battle of Dyram near Bath that the cities of Bath, Cirencester and Gloucester fell into enemy hands. Gower, of course, was far removed from the war zone, but in 584 two Saxon warlords advanced their armies towards south-east Wales. Meurig ap Tewdrig, King of Gwent Is-coed (southern Monmouthshire), was one of the petty kings of South Wales who fought the enemy at Tintern Ford, the result being that one Saxon warlord was killed and the other was forced to retreat in anger.

Meurig and the Monastery of St. Cenydd

Amongst the Llandaff Charters there are two land grants which record that Meurig married Onbrawst, daughter and heiress of Gwrgant the Great, of whom we know nothing other than he was the last independent king of Gower, for when he died his kingdom passed to Meurig. As with other kings of his day, Meurig and his entourage were frequently on the move, travelling from one royal estate to another, for not only did regular progresses keep him in touch with the *uchelwyr* of his now dispersed kingdom, but he was at liberty to demand food renders from the peasantry who worked the estates that had formerly belonged to his father-in-law. It was probably during one of his progresses through Gower in the first decade of the 7th century that Meurig put his name to the following charter.

> Be it known to us that Meurig ap Tewdrig, King of Glywysing [?], and his wife, Onbrawst, daughter of Gwrgant the Great, has given to God and Oudoceus, the Bishop ... three modii [27 acres] of land at Cilcinhinn [exact location unknown, but

evidently in Gower] and six modii [54 acres] of land at Conuoy; that is Lanngenei [Llangenydd] and also Llandeilo Talybont [the bounds of which encircled land on both sides of the River Loughor].

This charter provides the earliest reference to a monastery dedicated to St. Cenydd (Llangenydd), a holy man who has stronger links with Gower than any other saint. According to legend, Cenydd had been born crippled and consigned to a wicker basket, which was set adrift in the Loughor Estuary. When sea birds snatched him from the waves, they took him to Worm's Head where they protected him while an angel brought a miraculous bell of brass, which had a teat. Thus Cenydd is said to have been fostered until he was able to hobble. He led the life of a hermit for 18 years. Then the angel took him to the Island of Burry Holms where he constructed a cell of osiers and an oratory where a heavenly host frequently conversed with him. When he died he was buried, apparently, on the island. A fairy tale, surely? Or is there a grain of truth in the story?

In the late 11th century one Caradog joined the court of Rhys ap Tewdwr, King of Deheubarth (1079-93) to take charge of the king's favourite dogs. Through negligence, Caradog lost the dogs and had to flee to Llandaff where he became a monk. About 1100, Herewald, Bishop of Llandaff (d.1104), sent Caradog to Gower, not to the mainland Church of Llangenydd (where Herewald had ordained four priests in succession), but to Burry Holms where, as a hermit, Caradog built himself a hut near

Burry Holms where St. Cenydd is said to have lived the life of a hermit.

a graveyard. It took Caradog three days to clear the graveyard and, in doing so, he found the grave of St. Cenydd. He, then, built a wooden church within the graveyard; two decades later this church was referred to in a charter of c.1119 as 'the Church of the Isle'.

As a 'holy and religious man', Caradog became well known in his day, his name appearing in several manuscripts relating to the 12th century, but can his connection with Burry Holms be verified? What has been revealed by excavation on the lower, eastern end of the island during the late 1960s is the remains of a 12th-century stone church, beneath which were post-holes of an earlier wooden structure. One of the post-holes had penetrated an earlier burial. Could this have been the grave of St. Cenydd? Apparently not, for his bones were removed to Bardsey Island in North Wales soon after the discovery of his grave; moreover, what has been revealed by excavation is that the burial penetrated by a post-hole was one of several, most of them within an enclosure consisting of an earthen bank surmounted by a palisade. These findings confirm that a wooden church, little more than 3m. square, had been built within the graveyard; they also confirm that, just outside the graveyard, there had been a circular hut, apparently of the same date as the wooden church. The posts of the church were later removed in order to erect the stone church.

To return to King Meurig's charter, which refers to a gift of 54 acres 'at Conuoy; that is, Lanngenei'. The acreage was undoubtedly on the mainland as the island is only 15 acres, and the charter describes the bounds of the gifted land as 'from the ridge of the mountain dividing the wood and plain by the sea, as far as the source of Diuguarch, following it down to the sea'. The later charter of c.1119 confirms the existence of church property in the vicinity of the mainland 'Church of St. Kenetus'; that is, Llangenydd. The Burry Holms site was evidently used as a place of retreat, for a grant of 1429 describes the site as 'the hermitage of St. Kenydd-atte-Holmes'.

A New Language

From 410 onwards the language of the Gauls gradually died out, whereas the language of the *Britanni* underwent a significant change so that, by the latter half of the 6th century, a new language had come into being—a primitive form of Welsh—by which time the *Britanni* were referring to themselves as the *Combrogi*, meaning 'Countrymen', the modern equivalent of which is *Cymry*. It was during the late 6th century that the earliest known literary works of the *Combrogi* were composed. These works, which have survived in the language of a later age, are all in verse; they recount the bitter fighting that took place in the North of England, providing us with the names of Urien Rheged and other heroic kings. The men who composed these works—Talhaearn, Taliesin, Llywarch Hen, Aneirin—prompt a reconsideration of one of the oldest institutions of the Celtic world.

The Bards

Lyric poets were as much a part of Celtic society as the craftsmen who fashioned ornamented iron swords for a warrior aristocracy. The Bard, Taliesin, is known for his
praise of Urien Rheged, a warrior king who, in the late 6th century, appears to have
ruled all the land west of the Pennines and who came close to annihilating his German
neighbours. Urien's people were known as *Gwyr o'r gogledd*, meaning 'Men of the
North'. *Gwyr* is also the word—or name—from which English *Gower* is derived. It is,
therefore, easy to see how the word *Gwyr* could lead to misunderstanding. Centuries
after Urien's death the poetry about him became acceptable to Norman-French ears,
except that their minstrels called him Urien of *Goire*, which is not unlike *Gwyr*. By the
16th century the Bards of West Wales were making capital out of the similarity in the
words *Goire* and *Gwyr*, claiming a connection between Urien Rheged and Gower.
Whenever an *uchelwr* wished to trace his ancestors he turned to the Bards who, apart
from being poets, were the acknowledged experts on genealogy, and they, in their
efforts to please patrons, saw no wrong in linking their patrons with heroes long dead,
Urien of *Gwyr* being one of them.

Further Misunderstandings

The fact that English colonists established themselves in Gower during the 12th
century is reason, at this point, to consider who these people were and where they
came from. It is also necessary to eradicate further misunderstandings. When the
Combrogi spoke of their Germanic neighbours they used the word *Saesneg* (Saxons)
to apply to them all, irrespective of whether they were Angles, Saxons, Jutes, Frisians
or any other ethnic group from northern Europe. The Saxons on the other hand often
referred to their Celtic neighbours as the *Cumber*, as in Cumberland, which was their
way of saying *Combrogi*. More frequently they used variations of the term *Welisc*,
meaning 'foreigner', which later developed into Welsh.

Of all the Germanic people to settle in *Britanniae* the Angles were by far the
most numerous, coming from Schleswig and northern Germany in such numbers that
the historian, Procopius, reported an empty land between the Slavs and the Varni of
Denmark. These Angles, or *Englisc* as they called themselves, settled in East Anglia, in
Lincolnshire and Leicestershire, in south Yorkshire and Northumberland, places from
whence they spread westwards in the late 6th to early 7th century to create the
powerful kingdoms of Northumbria and Mercia. By the 7th century all the Germanic
people of *Britanniae* seem to have regarded themselves as *Englisc*.

A Conquered People

From *c.*580 onwards the North of England and the west Midlands became the stage
for a bloody, protracted struggle that was to last almost 80 years. By 660 the North of
England was all but lost, the *Combrogi* holding out in Cumberland and in the Scottish
Lowlands where they united to form the Kingdom of Strathclyde. To the south, the
west Midlands fell into enemy hands, the frontier rolled back to the borders of Wales.

There are many reasons to explain why the *Combrogi*, who must have originally outnumbered their *Englisc* neighbours, came to lose control of so much territory. For example, it could be argued that only a minority of the *Combrogi*—the free men— were permitted to fight, whereas the *Englisc* were a nation in arms, but the question that needs to be addressed—if only because history would repeat itself in Gower—is what became of the *Combrogi* whose lands passed into enemy hands?

At one time it was believed that they were driven westwards, but Wales and Dumnonia (Cornwall, Devon and part of Somerset) could never have supported an enlarged population—the size and nature of these regions, and more so the climate, would not have permitted it; there was just not enough cultivable land to go round. Another hypothesis is that the *Combrogi* were exterminated. Yet the same Germanic people settled in France and they did not annihilate the Gaulish population there. There is, of course, irrefutable evidence that appreciable numbers of *Combrogi* migrated to Brittany and to Galatica in north-west Spain, and there are suggestions that some may have sailed to Ireland, in which case others must surely have moved into Wales, Cumberland, Strathclyde and Dumnonia, but those who pulled up stakes were, as always, the free men. The unfree stayed where they were to serve new masters, to adopt a new language, a new cultural identity. What has been said about genes supports the idea that large numbers of *Combrogi* became *Englisc*. In some areas they lost their cultural identity within a few generations; in other places they survived until the 11th century and later; moreover, the notion of assimilation can be supported by the extant *Englisc* laws of Kent and Wessex which have provisions for both privileged and peasant *Welisc*, although there are many who would contest the evidence of these laws.

The *Taeogion*

It has been suggested that the *Combrogi* peasantry—the unfree people who made it possible for the free men to live in comparative ease—were descended from the pre-Celtic people of the Neolithic Age, although there is no evidence to support this. In South Wales these people were known as *taeogion*; they were bound to the soil on which they lived and worked, which they could not leave without the landowners consent; if the land was sold, then they became subject to a new land-lord. They were considered to be inferior, for their life, honour and property were worth considerably less than the life, honour and property of free men. It is possible they carried arms for personal protection, and in North Wales during the late 13th century there is evidence to suggest they fought for Llywelyn ap Gruffudd and Madoc ap Llywelyn, but according to extant lawbooks of the 13th century their military obligations were to attend to baggage trains and carry out camp duties, for in times of war all *taeog* communities were obliged to furnish one man, one axe and one packhorse. Despite these handicaps the *taeogion* could escape from bondage if, with the concurrence of their lord, they took up a profession such as that of a smith, bard or cleric, although the enfranchisement did not extend to a son unless

The Mardy Hotel, Gorseinion, site of a taeog *community named Rhyd-y-maerdy.*

he likewise took up the profession; moreover, a *taeog* community could be set free if, with the lord's permission, a church was established in their locality.

A *taeog* community that was sited on land belonging to a king was usually known as a *maerdref* or *maerdy*—meaning the *maer's* hamlet—which took its name from a royal officer known as the *maer*, who was responsible for telling the *taeogion* what to grow and where. The names of several *maerdrefi* have survived in the northern half of Gower—for example, Maerdy is the name of a present-day hamlet about a mile south of Ammanford. Another Maerdy can be found near Blaen-nant-hir, at Grid Reference 725 115, and there was a Rhyd-y-maerdy at Gorseinion, the name preserved in the present-day Mardy Hotel. The public house at Clydach known as The Vardre is a corruption of *Y Faerdref*, and a 14th-century account provides additional evidence that a *taeog* community had existed there as well, although, by then, the *maerdrefi* of Gower had ceased to function as royal estates, the *taeogion* having become rent-paying tenants. A later survey suggests that another bond community had existed at Neuaddwen, near Garnant. There must have been many more *taeog* communities in Gower that have left no trace, espe-cially in the Peninsula, and the fact must not be overlooked that the *uchelwyr* also had their *taeogion*, although the records for South Wales are silent about them. The *taeogion* were certainly the most numerous class, for the *Domesday Survey* of 1086-7 records that, in the border areas of Wales, 52% of the native population were classified as bond tenants. In King Meurig's day the percentage was probably much higher.

Slaves

In the Dark Ages, slavery in Wales was the norm, continuing as such into the 14th century and beyond. The majority of these unfortunates were slaves by birth, though in origin some of them may have been captives from cross-border raids as is suggested by a Saxon woman who, about 740, was given as part-payment for land. Slaves were accounted as chattels, to be bought and sold for the price, in later centuries, of four cows. That is not to say that they had absolutely no life of their own, for slaves in Wales are known to have purchased their freedom, which suggests that some, at least, were able to acquire property, even wealth, and may have held important positions in the households of kings and *uchelwyr*. Our only indication as to what percentage of the population were slaves comes from the *Domesday Survey* of 1086-7, which records that 17% of the population in the border areas of Wales were either slaves or oxmen. The percentage is likely to have been higher in the Dark Ages.

Kings, Charters and Church Property

By marriage or war, Meurig and his descendants gradually annexed the petty king-doms of south-east Wales so that, by the early 8th century, there was but one kingdom—Glywysing—which spread over the pre-1974 counties of Glamorgan, Monmouthshire and southern Herefordshire. About the middle of the 7th century, Meurig was succeeded by his two sons, Arthrwys and Idnerth, though it does not necessarily mean that the kingdom was divided, for it seems to have been the practice in Glywysing that several kings could share power, one of whom may have been pre-eminent. Arthrwys appears in one of the Llandaff Charters in connection with a dispute over church property in Gower. The charter reads:

> It is well known that Bishop Oudoceus acquired land of his own, that is the estate of Cingualan [in Gower] which St. Oudoceus lost from the time of the mortality; that is the yellow plague until the time of Arthrwys ap Meurig. [And] after great contention between Bishop Oudoceus [or more likely one of his successors] and Bivan, Abbot of Illtud [Llanilltud Fawr] who said the land was his, the aforesaid land was at last ... adjudged to St. Oudoceus. [The charter suggests that the estate of Cingualan comprised of] the cell of Cynwalan with all its land, and the cells of Arthfodu, Ceinwyrig and Pencreig [this last cell may be connected with Penycraig in the parish of Llanrhidian]. [It would appear that the] cell of Cynwalan with all its land [was the most important part of the estate and its bounds were given as:] Below the ditches [streams] at the sea, following the two ditches to the mountain, along it to the ridge of the boundary of Lanngenei, which puts us in mind of part of the parish of Rhosili.

The 'cell of Cynwalan' developed into a monastery, according to a 10th-century charter, and a Llancynwalan was mentioned in an early 12th-century papal bull along with several other church properties in Gower.

Morgan ab Arthrwys succeeded his father in the later half of the 7th century; about 695, according to the Llandaff Charters, he took:

possession of the Church of Cyngur Trosgardi, which heretofore belonged to Teilo ... and restored it ... to all the pastors of Llandaff forever ... with all its territory and bounds, and with Merwallt ... prince of that church ... and granted to the Church and its territory, and to the inhabitants ruling and dwelling there autonomy without governor or sub-governor ... and without attending warlike expeditions either within the country, or without.

What this meant is that the Church of Cyngur Trosgardi (which probably stood on the site of the present-day parish church of Bishopston) had originally been dedicated to an otherwise unknown saint named *Cyngur*. When the charter was drawn up, *Merwallt,* 'prince of that church', had been abbot there; this is interesting in that a papal bull of 1119 gives the name of the church as *St. Teilo de Llanferwallt*—St. Teilo being the second known bishop of Llandaff and *Merwallt* the earliest recorded abbot of what, in King Morgan's day, had been a monastery. As to the monastery's 'territory and bounds' the charter recorded them in detail, and almost 100 years ago a local historian, C.A. Seyler, presented a convincing argument that the 'bounds' in the charter corresponded to those of the present-day parish of Bishopston, except for the later addition of Manselfield. Within these 'bounds' the church and the local inhabitants enjoyed a degree of autonomy without having to answer to any 'governor or sub-governor' (presumably of Gower); this clause was to determine Bishopston's status throughout the Middle Ages. The last-mentioned clause concerning 'warlike expeditions' shows that *Merwallt* and his predecessors had been obliged to furnish men to accompany the kings of Glywysing on forays, a not unusual occurrence as bishops and abbots considered themselves on a par with kings and princes, often travelling in the company of armed retinues even as late as the 12th century. The clause makes it plain that a military obligation was attached to the privilege of holding land, and it would certainly have applied to all free men whose presence, when required, would have enlarged the king's warband.

Renders

From the time of Morgan ab Arthrwys the Llandaff Charters make it increasingly apparent that the kings of Glywysing did not depend solely upon plunder and tribute for provisions, but more so on food renders from their own subjects, both free and unfree. The kings' companions collected the renders not from individuals, but from territorial units, the most frequently mentioned being the *tref* (the *vill* in Latin documents) which, for the most part, appear to have been no more than a few scattered homesteads in which the men were probably related. The amount due from any particular *tref* varied according to location and whether the *tref* was free, unfree or even ecclesiastical. *Gwestfa*, for instance, was a once a year render from a *tref* occupied by free men. One half of a typical *gwestfa* was paid in the form of cereal and/or bread, one quarter in liquor, and the remaining quarter in flesh or dairy products. The only reference to *gwestfa* in Gower is in the receiver's account that has survived for the financial year 1366-7, which records that the free men of Kilvey were still paying *gwestfa* to the Anglo-Norman lords of Gower at that time.

The Celtic Church

Until fairly recently, writers referred to the so-called Celtic Church as if it were a church peculiar to the Celts. The truth is that certain practices relating to the Church in Celtic lands were once prevalent throughout Europe, but from the 7th century onwards, when the Celtic fringe became somewhat isolated, many of these practices lingered while the rest of Europe moved on. Consequently, there was a difference in the way the Celtic clergy tonsured their hair, their forehead shaven to a line extending from ear to ear as opposed to the Roman practice of shaving only the crown. At one time the Celtic clergy celebrated Easter on a different day to the one ordained by Rome. Another distinguishing feature about the Celtic Church was its use of the word 'saint', a term which applied to all clerics be they monks, priests or hermits, none of whom were officially canonized by Rome.

Pillar Stone, Llanmadog Church.

Yet another feature of the Celtic Church was the practice (originating in southern France) of erecting pillar-stones that are distinguished by incised crosses. Two such stones are inside Llanmadog Church, both found in the churchyard and dated to the 7th to 9th centuries. A much older grave-marker has been set in the internal sill of one window, which bears an inscription in Roman capitals that reads: 'Of … Vectus, son of … Guanus; he lies here', and is dated to the early 6th century. The church also has the distinction of being associated with a Celtic hand-bell that was found in a nearby field. Llanmadog is undoubtedly an ancient church, yet it has no history prior to the 12th century.

Perhaps the most distinguishing feature about the Celtic Church is that, from the 8th century onwards, some of the larger monasteries seem to have become home to communities (*clasau*) consisting of an abbot and a body of canons (*claswyr*) who had a share in monastic income and property. Not all the *claswyr* were necessarily monks—some were laymen, and as both monks and laymen could marry, then their share in monastic property could be transmitted to children. In Gower only one monastery is known to have been in the hands of a *claswyr*.

The Monastery at Llangyfelach

In his *Life of St. David* (written *c.*1195) the author, Rhigyfarch, referred to Llangyfelach's former status as an important *monasterium* within the See of St. David's, claiming it to be where the saint received a portable alter from Jerusalem. This is one of the earliest references to Llangyfelach which, at that time, may have been no more than a parish church. Yet a monastery must have existed on the site at an earlier date because two 9th-century stone slabs have been discovered within the area enclosed by the churchyard wall, each with a cross carved into its surface, as well as the base of a 10th century pillar-cross.

St. Cyfelach is an unknown saint, but when his followers built a settlement at Llangyfelach they encircled it with a rubble wall to separate their world from the world beyond. An enclosed settlement such as this was known as a *llan*, and Rice Merrick, in his *Morganiae Archaiographia* of *c.*1578, mentions the existence of a ruinous structure at Llangyfelach called *Y Llan*; this probably followed the line of the present-day churchyard wall, which is circular and encloses quite a large area. Within *Y Llan* there would have been a small church (later dedicated to St. David), several circular huts called *cells* (providing accommodation for the monks and their families), a barn, possibly a *scriptorium* (a library) and no doubt a guest-house as the monastery prob-ably served as a stage with tracks converging on it from several directions. Rice Merrick also mentioned that, in his day, the episcopal manor of Llangyfelach was known as Clase, a name derived from *Clas* (the property of the *claswyr*). In 1815 the manor of Clase was said to have covered an area of 3,667 acres, extending from Penllergaer to the Tawe River, and from Fforest Newydd to what was once Mynydd-bach School.

The *Cymry*

There is a hiatus in our knowledge of Gower during the 8th and 9th centuries, but its people are unlikely to have felt threatened by the *Englisc* even though, to the south, the Dumnonii were confined to Cornwall from *c.*730 onwards. To the east, the *Englisc* border in the late 8th century became fixed on Offa's Dyke. The dyke was not a linguistic divide, more a political one, for the people on both sides of the dyke were speaking a language that is known to linguists as Old Welsh. This language had been slowly evolving from the late 6th century onwards, and the people who spoke it, including the inhabitants of Gower, were now calling themselves *Cymry*.

Names

Many of the personal names used by the *Cymry* from the 8th century onwards are familiar to modern Welshmen, but there were no surnames in the Dark Ages. Men with similar names were individualized by the use of *ap*—meaning 'son of'—followed by the name of their fathers, as in Meurig ap Tewdrig, or by *ab* when the father's name began with a vowel, as in Morgan ab Arthrwys. A man might also be identified by the addition of a nickname, as in Heilyn Goch, meaning 'Heilyn with the Red Hair'.

Yet another means of identifying men with similar names was to add their place of origin, as in Maelgwn Gwynedd, meaning 'Maelgwn of (or from) Gwynedd'. Women were usually distinguished by the use of *ferch*, meaning 'daughter of'. King Tewdrig's wife, for example, would have been known as *Onbrawst ferch Gwrgant Fawr*— 'Onbrawst the daughter of Gwrgant the Great'.

Appearance and Dress

The best description of the *Cymry* with regards to their appearance and dress is in the works of Gerald, and even though he wrote in the late 12th century his observations would apply to those who lived in at least the latter part of the Dark Ages. Gerald commented on their swarthy complexion which, he claimed, was due to their Trojan descent. He described them as 'light and active, hardy rather than strong', and mentions that both the men and women tonsured their hair in exactly the same way— cut 'close round to their ears and eyes'—a fashion that would have probably prevailed among the unfree as well. His only comments on women's dress was that they covered 'their heads with a large, white veil, folded together in the form of a crown' rather like a turban. Other items of dress are mentioned in the laws: a shift, meaning a straight, unwaisted dress, a mantle and shoes, although it is likely that most women went barefooted. The men, he claimed, shaved their beards, but kept their moustaches. Many of the men—and no doubt the women too—appear to have been red-haired, as is suggested by the frequency with which *coch* (red) is attached to personal names as in Heilyn Goch. With regards to dress, Gerald described a young prince as

> of fair complexion, with curled hair, tall and handsome, clothed only, according to custom ... with a thin cloak and inner garment, his legs and feet bare.

The dress of the more lowly *Cymry* is unlikely to have been any different. Indeed, drawings of 13th century soldiers confirm Gerald's observations, the inner garment— or tunic—in each case being long-sleeved and falling to just below the knee. Other drawings of similar date depict court officers wearing what appear to be voluminous breeches. Even when allowance is made for the favourable climate of the 12th and 13th centuries, the clothing of the *Cymry* appears to be unbelievably scant, and was seen as such by outsiders as they sometimes referred to the *Cymry* being accustomed to 'endure cold'. Only in the early part of the Dark Ages, when the climate was cold and wet, are there any references to coats of skins and other warm clothing.

The Vikings

Towards the end of the 8th century the Vikings—otherwise known as the Norsemen— began pillaging Europe before turning to conquest and colonization. The Swedish element moved south to lay the foundations of a kingdom called Russia. The Norwegians struck out into the Atlantic, establishing colonies as far afield as Newfoundland. The Danes swept across the North Sea to harry the *Englisc* in much the same way as the *Englisc* had harried the *Cymry*. In the late 9th century the Danes began settling in large numbers on the east coast; from there they set out to make England *Daneland* and would have succeeded had they not suffered a crushing defeat at the hand of Alfred, King of Wessex. By treaty, southern England and the west Midlands became Alfred's domain; the northern and eastern counties became Danelaw, its people subject to Danish kings. To the west, the Norwegians invaded Ireland in 839, establishing defended settlements at Dublin, Wexford and Waterford, but within a few years they were overwhelmed by the Danes. From Ireland the Vikings carried out their first recorded raid on Wales in 852; thereafter they harried the country relentlessly, although their attempts at conquest failed.

The Danes in Gower

Our only record of a Viking attack on Gower comes from the *Annales Cambriae*, which records that, in 986, the Danes burned the monastery of Llangenydd. The Vikings no doubt carried out several raids on the Peninsula, and there are many who would argue that they settled there, basing their claim on place-names that are said to be of Viking origin. Recent research has reduced the number of place-names that were believed to have originated from Old Norse to just two, one being Burry Holms 'holms' meaning 'island'.

The other place-name, Swansea, originated from *Sweyn's Ey—Sweyn* being a common Norse name and *Ey* meaning 'island or inlet'. The name first appears in abbreviated forms such as *Sven, Swensi*, etc, on ten or eleven coins dated to around 1140. In other words, the origin of the name Swansea cannot be traced back earlier than the 12th century and may, therefore, have originated in conjunction with the 12th century Anglo-Norman castle that was built near the Tawe Estuary. Other place-names such as Rother Sker, Langland, do not appear in ancient documents and may, therefore, be relatively modern.

Brooches of Viking origin have been found in the parishes of Llanmadog and Llangenydd; a glass bead of Norse origin was also discovered at Hen Gastell. To these finds can be added that the Revd. J.D. Davies in his *History of West Gower*, published in the late 19th century, recorded a number of Norse-related traditions associated with the area around Llangenydd. Unfortunately, these traditions are of a kind that were intended to explain the origin of place-names such as Tankeylake and should be regarded as of no great antiquity. All things considered, there is little evidence to support a Viking settlement in Gower beyond what may be associated with the Anglo-Norman settlement.

Exchange and English Currency

Throughout the 890s Danish armies were active in the west Midlands and in the border kingdoms of Wales; this led to an alliance between King Alfred and his successors and the petty kings of Wales. One advantage of this arrangement was that coins became available to the *Cymry*. After Roman coinage went out of use the *Cymry* had fallen back on a system of barter which they referred to as an exchange of gifts. By the 7th century the *Cymry* were expressing values in terms of bullion—so many ounces/pounds of silver or gold. By the 9th century they were making use of foreign, mostly *Englisc* silver pennies, and a hoard of 30 coins ascribed to Aethelraed II (current 1003-9) was found beneath stones at Penrice. Of course, bullion and coins were not available to everyone, and the Llandaff Charters make it plain that by the 7th century the *Cymry* were also expressing values in terms of so many cows (kine). Horses, for example, were valued at between three and twelve kine. At an unknown date the value of a cow became fixed at five shillings.

A Tyrant in Gower

When Gildas wrote of the kings of his day he accused five of them of crimes ranging from adultery to murder, all of them tyrants, he claimed, who thirsted for war and booty. Similar accusations could be levelled at the petty kings who ruled in the early 10th century. There were several members of Meurig's dynasty ruling in Glywysing at that time and one of them, Gruffudd ab Owain, appears to have been active in Gower about 925. According to the Llandaff Charters, Gruffudd committed three outrages

> against God and the saints, firstly by seizing Idmab ab Idcant in the monastery of St. Cynwal and violating refuge; secondly by slaying Cyfarherw ap Crashaion in the monastery of St. Ceinwyry, that is Llanberugall; thirdly by selling to some person, without leave of the bishop, Porthdulon, from the earliest time a church of Dubricius.

In an age of violence, King Gruffudd's outrages would not have been unusual occurrences, for even his ancestor, Meurig, committed murder, and the Llandaff Charters record many occasions when kings had to make restitution for acts of violence committed by them and by members of their retinues. It may be wondered why people accepted tyrants, but there was no alternative form of government, no democracy as is now known. A king was necessary to prevent anarchy, to provide leadership in times of war. In the case of King Gruffudd the Church obtained restitution—four *modii* (36 acres) of land in a place that cannot now be located.

What has been recorded about King Gruffudd confirms the existence of two of the four known Gower monasteries—those dedicated to St. Cynwal and St. Ceinwyry; the other two being Llangenydd and Llangyfelach. St. Cynwal's monastery, according to an earlier description of its bounds under the name of St. Cynwalan, would appear to have been at Rhosili, its location probably on the warren below and on the seaward side of Rhosili Down where, in Anglo-Norman times, a church is known to have existed. St. Ceinwyry's monastery, that is Llanberugall, is synonymous with the church of Cyngur Trosgardi and the Llanferwallt that existed at Bishopston. The last mentioned Porthdulon is relative to Gwordog's daughter, Dulon, and the 26 acres her father gave to Bishop Dubricius. The whereabouts of Porthdulon is unknown, although *porth* suggests a location near the sea or perhaps a ferry. It is believed to have been synonymous with St. Peter's Chapel in the Caswell Valley, but there is no proof of this. Whatever its location it still existed in the early 12th century when it was several times mentioned in papal bulls as Porthtulon.

The Laws of Hywel Dda

Between 942 and 949-50, Hywel Dda (Hywel the Good) ruled all Wales except for the south-east, an exceptional achievement for a *Cymro*, but what Hywel is remembered for most is for codifying the laws within his kingdom; that is, he arranged to have them committed to writing. These laws were customary laws, upheld by the free landowners, aided by professional lawyers, who gathered at what we would call the scene of the crime to take part in what was really a tribunal. In the Dark Ages, when kings played no part in law enforcement, the purpose of these tribunals was to avoid disruptive blood-feuds by bringing the parties together and ensuring that the injured party was suitably compensated by the perpetrator 'and his kinsmen'. In a society where kinship was of paramount importance, the kinsmen of the wrongdoers were held equally responsible and expected to contribute to the compensation. The clergy also had a role to play at these tribunals, providing the holy relics upon which men swore to tell the truth, and to impose a penance on the wrongdoers for serious offences. Only later, from the late 11th century onwards, did kings become increasingly involved in law and order, although in South Wales their role, or the role of their agents, was primarily that of arbitrators. That said, let us now touch upon one aspect of the law that existed in Wales and, therefore, in Gower as well.

Kindred Groups

The word *cenedl* is often found in extant manuscripts on Welsh law. Its modern meaning is 'nation', but in the latter part of the Dark Ages (when the term first appears in written form) it connoted a kindred-group of indeterminate extent. The lawbooks that have survived from *c.*1200 onwards make it plain that it was necessary, at times imperative, for free men and women to know exactly who were of kin to them and to what degree—for example, all persons interrelated within four degrees (those who were descended from a common great-grandfather in the male line) had a vested interest in matters pertaining to inheritance, particularly when it involved the property of a kinsman who had died without a son and heir; they also had a say in the marriage arrangements of a kinswoman.

Relationship within seven degrees could be just as important, for if a man committed manslaughter or murder, then in theory at least all who were related to him within seven degrees on the *spear* (father's) side and on the *distaff* (mother's) side were deemed equally responsible and were, therefore, liable to contribute towards compensating the dead man's *cenedl*, so as to ward off a disruptive blood-feud. Conversely, when a man was killed, intentionally or otherwise, then all who were related to him within seven degrees—on both the *spear* and *distaff* sides—received a share in the compensation, which was calculated according to the dead man's status. The life of an *uchelwr*, for example, was valued at between 126 and 252 kine.

A *cenedl* that was defined by degrees of kinship was not a permanent arrangement, but one in which kindred banded together for the sole purpose of settling a specific issue—rather like relatives today coming together when there is a death or marriage in the family. Once the issue had been resolved, then the members of a four or seven-degree *cenedl* went their separate ways. There was, however, another *cenedl* known as a *gwely* that had a more permanent existence, the members (*uchelwyr*) of which could trace their descent from a common ancestor in the male line; they were banded together primarily for the purpose of holding land.

The term *gwely* (literally 'bed' or 'resting place') appears in the earliest extant lawbooks of the late 12th and 13th centuries. By the early 14th century it becomes apparent that most *uchelwyr* held their land not simply as individuals, but also as members of a *gwely*. The average *gwely* might consist of 20 *uchelwyr*, but should the number approach 40 the *gwely* became unmanageable and tended to split into two or more smaller *gwelyau*. The purpose of banding together as a *gwely* was to keep land within the kindred group. Each member of a *gwely* held varying amounts of land, but none of them could sell or give away what belonged to them, nor could they devise any part of their land by will; nor could they deforest areas of woodland without the consent of other members of the *gwely*. It has already been said that, if a man died without a son and heir, his land passed to near relatives; that way the dead man's land remained within the *gwely*.

Gwelyau certainly existed in Gower in 1326, for a survey taken that year mentions that members of seven *gwelyau* held land within the episcopal manor of Clase (centred on Llangyfelach). The survey provided the ancestral names of the seven *gwelyau*—Ieaun ap Kedivor, Seyssill ap Gwyauan and so on. Although it was not stated in the survey, there can be no doubt that most of the land held by the seven *gwelyau* lay outside the manor for the simple reason that only 12 members of these kindred groups actually resided or held land within the said manor.

Additional evidence for the existence of *gwelyau* in Gower comes from an inquiry of 1319 into the illegal sale of land by the then Lord of Gower, William de Breos. The findings of the inquiry record that Hywel ap Gruffudd 'and his brethren' were one of three kindred groups to purchase property in an inland territory that was then known as *Supraboscus*. The purchase of Hywel 'and his brethren' was that of a holding known as *Traean Meibion Meurig*—literally 'the third part of the sons of Meurig'. Meurig evidently had three sons, each of whom inherited a 'third part' of their father's land. When William de Breos sold *Taean Meibion Meurig* (which, at the time, obviously belonged to him) it was occupied by Meurig's grandsons. It is, therefore, possible that Meurig and his descendants were all *taeogion*, holding their land as an unfree *gwely*, a not unusual arrangement as surveys carried out in the early 14th century show that more than half the unfree Welsh communities in North Wales were organized into *gwelyau*.

There is no historical references to *gwelyau* in the Peninsula, but recent research relating to old charters and the layout of fields and farms in certain areas revealed that *gwelyau* probably existed at Dunvant, Cilonnen and Three Crosses, which is unsurprising as these three locations are in an area that proved to be the last place in the Peninsula to lose its Welsh identity.

On the evidence that has been presented it would be tempting to think of the *Cymry* as a tribal society, but it must be understood that although a *gwely* was a grouping of related tribesmen, the holdings of its members were scattered, often intermingled amongst the holdings of related and unrelated *gwelyau*. A *gwely* certainly did not occupy a compact tribal area. The dispersed holdings of its members may be explained by the commonly held view that an ancestor had the permission of a king to settle himself and his household in a *tref* where he built a *hendre* (old homestead), then cleared the surrounding land for cultivation. When the ancestor died his property was divided equally between his sons, each of whom would have received a share in arable, meadow and wood, the youngest son inheriting the *hendre*. Partitioning of the land would have continued until such time as it became necessary for descendants to acquire additional land in neighbouring *trefi*—or even in neighbouring territories—at the same time retaining their inherited portions of land in the original *tref*. This is a simplified view of what must have been a complex development, the complexity made worse by the devastating effects of wars, famines and plagues.

Einion

After the death of Hywel Dda in 949-50, his kingdom fragmented and Wales, once more, became a land of warring kingdoms. Hywel's son, Owain, succeeded to the territory of the Demetae, the Kingdom of Deheubarth as it had become known, until advancing years forced him to hand over the reins to his son, Einion. In 970 and again in 977, Einion ravaged Gower, preliminaries perhaps to subjugating Glywysing which, by then, had been renamed Morgannwg—Morgan's Land—after King Morgan Hen who died in 974. Einion may have taken over Morgannwg, if only for a short time, for in 984 he was slain by the *uchelwyr* of Gwent, the most easterly of Morgannwg's provinces. Einion's brother, Maredudd, then succeeded to the Kingdom of Deheubarth, but in 992 his position was challenged by Einion's son, Edwin, who came with a Saxon host and 'ravaged all the territory of Maredudd in Deheubarth; that is, Ceredigion, Dyfed, Gower and Cydweli'. Gower, then, had ceased to be part of Morgannwg and, for the next 80 years or so, it is linked with two other territories— Cydweli and Ystrad Tywi, the latter of which comprised of Cantref Mawr and Cantref Bychan.

Battles for Supremacy

The events of 970, 977 and 992 are the earliest reliable references to Gower outside the Llandaff Charters. They appear in the *Brut y Tywysogion*—the Chronicle of the Princes—which, for the most part, provides terse statements about the military exploits of the petty kings of Wales. The *Brut* does not mention Gower again until 1095, but during the intervening years the entries for Wales as a whole are a catalogue

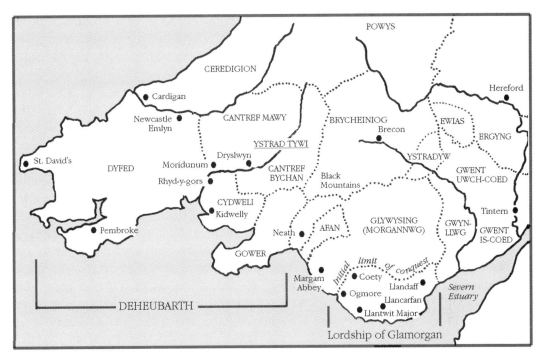

South Wales in the Dark Ages and early Anglo-Norman period.

of dynastic wars and mindless devastation, the purpose of which was to create a hegemony; that is, one kingdom having dominance over the others, thereby uniting the country under one powerful king. Gower being a frontier zone between the southern kingdoms of Deheubarth and Morgannwg would have seen armies come and go, but references to these advances can be found only in traditions, one of which states that the Einion who ravaged Gower in 970 and 977 also engaged his enemies near Cadle—meaning 'place of battle'—and was obliged to flee, only to be unhorsed in a bog that now bears his name—Gorseinion. Unfortunately, the story appears to be another attempt to explain the origin of place-names and is probably of no great antiquity.

Another tradition states that:

> the western tribes, defeated at Cadle after the death of their leader, who died of wounds whilst drinking at a well which still bears his name, fled in confusion towards the nearest ford of the River Loughor, and were routed a second time on the plains of Garn Goch [Red Stones] which took its name from the bloodshed which occurred there.

The well, which bears the name of the dead leader, is Llyn Cadwgan, located near Llewitha Bridge, Fforestfach. The tradition may be another fabrication, based perhaps on an entry in the Llandaff Charters which record that, during the reign of William the Conqueror (1066-87), a King Cadwgan ruled Gower, Cydweli and Cantref Bychan for many years until his death. Whatever the truth, the culmination of dynastic strife was that, between 1055-63, Gruffudd ap Llywelyn, King of Gwynedd, established a hegemony over the whole of Wales.

The Shrinking World of the *Cymry*

Moves towards unification had been going on in England and Scotland as well. The *Cymry* of Cornwall had been absorbed into the Kingdom of Wessex in the 10th century, although their language did not die out until the end of the 18th century. England became a unified kingdom in 937, and remained so even when ruled by Danish kings between 1013 and 1035. The unification of Scotland was more complicated in that it involved at least three different cultures. The Scottish Highlands had been occupied by a people known to the Romans as *Picti* (Picts), whose language appears to have been related to that of the *Britanni*, but from the 4th century onwards the Irish, whom the Romans had called *Scotti* (Scots), began colonizing the Western Isles and Kintyre from where they gradually extended their control over the *Picti* until, in 840, the *Picti* and the *Scotti* merged under a Scottish king to become the Kingdom of Albany. As the Gaelic of the *Scotti* was the language of both the court and the Church it eventually became the language of the Scottish Highlands. Then, when the last king of Strathclyde died in 1018, the *Cymry* of Lowland Scotland became part of Albany. By the 14th century the Lowland *Cymry* were speaking Gaelic, which finally gave way to *Inglis*. Elsewhere, the descendants of the *Britanni* were independent only in Cumberland, Wales and Brittany.

A New Threat—the Anglo-Normans

When Gruffudd ap Llywelyn was slain by his followers in 1063 the hegemony that he had created disintegrated and Wales once more became a land of warring kingdoms, so much so that, divided and devastated, it was ill prepared to counter the advances of a new people who had taken control of England, for in 1066 William, Duke of Normandy, dubbed 'the Conqueror', defeated the *Englisc* at the Battle of Hastings, wiping out a large proportion of the *Englisc* aristocracy, which he replaced with men from Normandy, the Low Countries and Brittany. The Normans were the most numerous of William's supporters. They were the descendants of Norsemen who had established themselves in Normandy in the 10th century and who, subsequently, adopted French as their language, which resulted in a distinctive Norman-French dialect. The Normans who settled in England after 1066—the Anglo-Normans as they are now known—became a select class, and although their numbers were relatively small when compared to the English, Norse and Celtic people of England, they nevertheless had a tremendous effect on the people they had conquered. They established a new order, they retained their language, and the fact that they invariably held positions of authority throughout the land led to their Norman-French dialect becoming the language not only of the nobility, but of the court, the lawcourts and the Church hierarchy which, in turn, led to numerous French words being incorporated into the Old English language.

Further Attacks on the *Cymry*

Among the warring factions in South Wales was one Caradog ap Gruffudd, King of Gwynllwg (in eastern Morgannwg). In 1072 he won a battle that led to him becoming ruler not only of Morgannwg, but also of Gower, Cydweli and the eastern half of Ystrad Tywi; that is, Cantref Bychan. The return of Gower to its former political association may, however, have been short-lived, for in 1081 Caradog fell at the Battle of Mynydd Carn in northern Dyfed (Pembrokeshire). One of his opponents, Rhys ap Tewdwr, became King of Deheubarth, which meant that in all probability Gower was again incorporated into the kingdom of West Wales.

Rhys ap Tewdwr had a troublesome reign, several times having to fight off rival dynasties, and on one occasion had to recruit Danish and Irish mercenaries to defeat his enemies. While all this was going on the Anglo-Normans were making inroads into the border kingdoms of South Wales and were claiming overlordship over both Powys and Gwynedd in North Wales. Further north, the Conqueror's son and successor, William Rufus, launched a devastating attack on Cumberland in 1092 and, from then on, Anglo-Norman and *Englisc* settlement was carried out on a scale that led to the language of the Cumberland *Cymry* dying out in the 14th century; worse was to follow.

During the winter of 1092-93, William Rufus is believed to have made plans for a similar invasion of South Wales, but in the spring of 1093 the Anglo-Norman, Bernard de Neufmarché, who had already gained a foothold in Brycheiniog, precipitated the invasion by resuming his offensive against the *Cymry* of that land. The offensive was seen by Rhys ap Tewdwr as threatening to Deheubarth, but when he responded to the threat he was killed near Brecon, leaving Deheubarth without a leader. In May the petty kings of Powys plundered Dyfed, presumably on behalf of their overlord, the Earl of Shrewsbury, for in July Anglo-Norman troops from Shrewsbury swept through the mountain passes of mid-Wales to overran Ceredigion and Dyfed where they established castles at Cardigan, Pembroke and elsewhere. It was about this time that the lowlands of Morgannwg were seized by another Anglo-Norman, Robert fitzHamo. By the end of the year the greater part of Wales was in enemy hands. It was all over bar the shouting—or so it seemed.

Then, early in 1094, when William Rufus was in Normandy, a revolt broke out in Gwynedd that spread like wildfire throughout Wales, the rebels ravaging enemy-held lands, storming castles and inflicted bloody reverses on Anglo-Norman troops whenever they caught them unawares—this was guerrilla warfare at its worst; it was a war in which no quarter was given, nor was any place spared, for in 1095 Anglo-Norman troops 'ravaged Ystrad Tywi, Cydweli and Gower' to the extent that 'they remained waste'. By 1098 the fighting abated, the Anglo-Normans claiming victory over a people who would not remain subservient for long.

The Last Years of Freedom

Henry I had reigned two years when, in 1102, Robert de Bellême, Earl of Shrewsbury, and his brother, Arnulf, Lord of Pembroke, were accused of plotting treason. Henry advanced on Robert's territory and, with the intention of detaching the Earl from the Welsh kings who were his vassals, offered one Iorwerth of Powys a great deal of territory, portions of which were Ystrad Tywi, Cydweli and Gower. After the revolt had been put down, Henry went back on his promise and gave Ystrad Tywi, Cydweli and Gower to one Hywel ap Goronwy. Henry's next move was to frustrate Hywel ap Goronwy, which he did in 1105 by ordering Richard fitzBaldwin to repair the ruined castle at Rhyd-y-gors—believed to have been sited about a mile south of Carmarthen, on the east bank of the Tywi.

Ruined or not, Rhyd-y-gors stood within Hywel's territory, the keeping of which the King had entrusted to him—at least that is what is implied by an entry in the *Brut* that says: 'And Hywel ap Goronwy, to whom the King had entrusted the keeping of Ystrad Tywi and Rhyd-y-gors'. Cydweli and Gower are not mentioned, but it may be that, as the King's agent, Hywel had adopted the title of Lord of Ystrad Tywi, the largest of the three territories in his charge. The rest of the entry records, somewhat confusingly, that Hywel took action against the foreigners who had settled in the vicinity of Rhyd-y-gors, presumably after he had tried unsuccessfully to obtain redress from the King. His retaliatory action made him a marked man, for the following year (1106) he 'was slain through the treachery of the French [the Anglo-Normans] who were keeping Rhyd-y-gors'. The *Brut* records:

> And It was Gwgan ap Meurig, the man (uchelwr) who had nurtured a son of Hywel, the man in whom Hywel placed greater trust than in anyone, who deceived him, for Gwgan invited him to his house, then sent to the French in the castle, informing them of the night and what place. And they came by night about cock-crow, surrounded the hamlet and the house, then raised a shout around the house. Hywel vigorously arose, reaching for his arms and calling his companions, but the sword, which he had placed above his head, and the spear, which he had placed below his feet, Gwgan had removed while he was asleep. So Hywel sought his companions, thinking they were ready to fight along with him, but they had fled at the first shout. Then he too fled, and Gwgan pursued him and did not give up until he caught him as he had promised the French. When Gwgan's companions had come to him they strangled Hywel and dragged him, well-nigh dead, to the French who cut off his head and took it to the castle.

Ystrad Tywi, Cydweli and Gower were now leaderless, open to attack, as Deheubarth had been 13 years earlier—it was to seal Gower's fate, render it open to settlement by yet another cultural group.

CHAPTER IV
The Anglo-Normans

Gower—a Commote

In the late 11th century, when kings sought to improve upon the collection of renders and became increasingly involved in law and order, the older units of territorial administration—the *cantrefi*—were divided into smaller, more manageable units called commotes. The word commote comes from Old English *mote* or *moot*, meaning an assembly of free men who met to discuss matters pertaining to their community. The Welsh equivalent of a commote (*cymwd*) developed into a territory in which functionaries were responsible for the fiscal and judicial interests of the kings. According to a jury that deliberated at Swansea in 1306, Gower had been a commote, one of three that constituted a larger territorial unit that appears in later sources as Cantref Eginog, the other two commotes being Cydweli and its eastern subdivision, Carnwyllion. If the territorial grouping is correct, then Cantref Eginog must have existed before 1116 because, by then, Gower, Cydweli and Carnwyllion were in Anglo-Norman hands. At an unknown, perhaps later date, Gower appears to have been subdivided into two commotes because a document of 1324 states that the Anglo-Norman lord, William de Breos, 'recovered the two commotes of Uwch-coed and Is-coed which constituted the whole of Gower'.

In view of its border position between two warring kingdoms, Gower may have been placed in the hands of territorial lords who had authority to summon the free men to arms. In his *Morganiae Archaiographia*, written almost 500 years after the event, Rice Merrick claimed that 'Rhydderch the Great' had been 'the last lord of Gower of the [Welsh] before it was conquered by the Strangers' (the Anglo-Normans). Unfortunately, Rhydderch's existence cannot be corroborated; even the claim that Gower was 'conquered' has to be treated with caution. There are several references to the conquest of Gower in documents that were compiled long after the event, all of them somewhat questionable claims, reason for some historians to suggest that the Anglo-Norman intrusion was a relatively peaceful affair. The suggestion is flawed for several reasons, one being that the scale of usurpation and colonization that took place in the coastal areas could not have been achieved without a measure of force.

At the very least heavily-armed horsemen can be imagined displacing the natives at lance-point, shouting at foot soldiers to bundle them out of their homes.

Welsh Warriors

Land was a free Welshman's most valuable asset, for with land went privileges, and the more land a man had the greater his prestige; moreover, the free men were tenacious, a trait confirmed by Henry ll, King of England (1154-89), when he mentioned in a letter to the Emperor of Constantinople that:

> In a certain part of this island there are a people called Welsh, so bold and ferocious that ... they do not fear to encounter an armed body of men, being ready to shed their blood for their country, to sacrifice their lives for renown.

Nothing highlights the differences between the free men and the Anglo-Normans than their respective modes of warfare. The free men were organized into warbands up to several hundred strong. According to Gerald, their leading men —be they petty kings, territorial lords or *uchelwyr*—went to war on 'swift and generous steeds', armed primarily with lances, the more influential wearing helmets, short coats of mail and high boots of untanned leather, whereas the rank and file majority were bare-footed and lightly-armed foot soldiers, of whom no finer description can be found than the one provided by a Breton who observed their warlike activities in France in 1196:

> The Welsh resort to the woods and are easily angered, skilful in marching through intricate ways, not hampered by footwear or leggings; they are taught to endure cold, never inclined to give up toil. Wearing a short tunic, no armour, they carry a sole weapon—a pike, battle-axe, bow, lance, a few hunting spears or javelins. They rejoice in plunder and bloodshed, and it is rare that any of them die except from wounds. If anyone throws it upon them that one of their kinsmen died without killing someone, they consider it a dishonour. They drink a milky substance, eating cheese and half-cooked flesh, the blood of which they squeeze out by pressing the meat in the cleft of a tree. They slaughter pitilessly, young and old, parents and children.

What has so far been said about the free men in the 12th century holds good for the preceding Dark Ages and, with the exception of the lance, their mode of fighting may have remained unchanged since Iron Age times. Usually, they were no match for heavily-armed troops on open ground, but they had the ability to make use of difficult terrain, to ambuscade in places that robbed the enemy of their superiority in arms; when they attacked they did so in a manner that was meant to confound their enemies in the onset. Gerald gave a graphic account of them when he wrote:

> In war this nation is severe in the first attack, terrible by their clamour and their appearance, filling the air with horrid shouting and the deep-toned clangour of long horns, swift in their advance, frequently throwing darts (short throwing spears). Bold in the onset, they cannot bear to be repulsed, being thrown into confusion the

moment they turn their backs; then they fly for safety without attempting to rally—but though driven to flight one day, they are ready to resume fighting on the next ... they are as easily overcome in a single battle as they are difficult to subdue in a protracted war.

Gower lent itself to ambuscades, for the subdivisions of *Uwch-coed* and *Is-coed*— meaning 'higher' and 'lower woods' respectively—suggest that the commote was still cloaked in woodland, a wilderness in which rivers did not flow between raised banks, but spread over the surrounding landscape, creating treacherous marshlands, especially around the lower reaches of the Tawe, Loughor, Llan and Lliw rivers and at Crymlyn to the east of Kilvey Hill. Wild animals such as stags, hinds, wild boars, martens and wolves are all mentioned in documents relating to the 12th century. The wolf probably died out in the 13th century, the wild boar in the 15th as one huge specimen is said to have been killed in the forest of Clyne around 1400. Red and roe deer, both protected by the nobility for pleasurable pursuit, continued to roam in woods and hills till at least the 16th century. Fishing rights are also mentioned in charters relating to the Tawe River, Pwllcynon and Swansea Bay where porpoise and sturgeon are specifically mentioned in a late 12th century charter, and an account for the year 1400 records an obligation to pay the lord of Gower 8d. for every salmon caught in the Tawe. As to the native Welsh, at the turn of the 12th century their numbers were still relatively small. There were no towns; the only nucleated settlements were the *maerdrefi* and possibly a territorial lord's court. From an outsider's point of view Gower was a land crying out for resettlement.

The Anglo-Normans

By 1116 the King of England had portioned out Ystrad Tywi, Cydweli and Gower to favourites, both Anglo-Norman and Welsh, in all probability granting them 'rights of conquest' to deter others from marching on the said territories. It seems fairly certain that the man who had Gower was an Anglo-Norman, Henry de Newburgh, Earl of Warwick, who, according to the *Brut*, was also 'called Henry (de) Beaumont'. There is no record as to how he acquired Gower, but even if his intrusion had been a relatively peaceful affair, it would still have been necessary for him to make good the King's mandate with a show of force. It would, of course, have been normal practice for a man of his standing to delegate the march on Gower to lesser men who, in times of war, served as heavily-armed horsemen—not knights in the accepted sense, but earthy men-at-arms, most of them Anglo-Normans. These lesser men were to replace the *uchelwyr* as the principal landowners in certain parts of Gower, and in order to obtain a clear understanding of the Anglo-Norman settlement it is, therefore, necessary to consider the men-at-arms more closely.

A man-at-arms could be identified by the fact that he wore a hauberk—a short-sleeved, knee-length shirt of chain-mail, slit from the waist down, front and back, to enable him to ride a horse. A hauberk afforded protection against sword slashes, even arrows, providing the wearer had a padded leather jerkin beneath it to cushion impact, although a hefty blow could still break bones. The nose guard on his domed helmet made him fearsome to behold; his shield was of wood, the rim bound by iron, kite-shaped and of sufficient length to protect his left side from shoulder to knee. He had little to fear from the men of Gower—unless his horse fell—for several decades were to pass before the Welsh made use of longbows to penetrate chain-mail. His weaponry consisted of a sword, lances, and sometimes a mace.

A man-at-arms had several horses—two heavy chargers, a riding horse and packhorses to carry a pavilion and his armour when not in use. He was accompanied by as many as three retainers—youths, mounted and lightly armed, who served a lengthy apprenticeship until, at about seventeen, they received the ceremonial slap on the face or neck that signified they had ascended to the rank of a man-at-arms. Apart from waiting on their masters, these young men could act as light cavalry, well-suited for pursuit. Obviously, a train such as this was costly and a man-at-arms with insufficient means had to place himself in the employ of a lord who would furnish him with horses and equipment, or else he had to acquire land to enable him to finance his own requirements.

In war the task of the men-at-arms was to advance on the enemy, either on foot or on horseback, and break the opposing formation to allow supporting foot soldiers to press the advantage home. They were also supported by archers who, in the onset, discharged their arrows, *en masse*, so that they rained upon the enemy, causing confusion and casualties. Chroniclers frequently omitted to mention foot soldiers, but they usually outnumbered the men-at-arms by at least ten to one, most of them English hirelings armed with spiked weapons and wearing some form of body protection. Camp followers such as sutlers and blacksmiths provided logistical support, but what Beaumont's men-at-arms lacked when they made towards unfamiliar territory was the expertise to contend with free men who fought by a different set of rules.

The Marcher Lords

The only people with experience in fighting the Welsh were the Marcher lords, men who held land on the Welsh border and in the conquered parts of Wales. In the Vale and foothills of what had become the Anglo-Norman Lordship of Glamorgan there were Marcher lords at hand to be of service—for a price—and two of them, William de Londres, Lord of Ogmore, and Payn de Turberville, Lord of Coety, may have been involved in the seizure of Gower as the descendants of both men are known to have held land in the Peninsula. These two lords—and any men-at-arms they may have raised from the Lordship of Glamorgan—would have been similarly equipped as the men-at-arms sent by Beaumont, but they differed in that they had adapted to combating the Welsh and, according to Gerald, were 'skilful on horseback, quick on foot' and accustomed to 'living in a constant state of warfare'; the Marcher lords also made use of Welsh levies.

Conquest

The men responsible for carrying out Beaumont's wishes may have advanced on Gower from the Vale of Glamorgan, or made their approach by sea, landing at Abertawe—meaning the mouth of the River Tawe. They may even have converged on the commote as a result of a combined land-sea operation. Whether they encountered opposition from the locals, aided perhaps by the men of Cydweli and Ystrad Tywi, is unknown, but the evidence for Wales as a whole indicates that Anglo-Norman conquests were usually piecemeal affairs in which earls and barons laid claim to relatively small territories such as commotes and *cantrefi*. Sometimes they plundered a small territory as a preliminary to constructing a major castle from which they terrorized the natives into submission. In many areas the natives countered with ambuscades and night attacks, and sporadic warfare such as this could last for decades until, eventually, both sides reached an agreement—albeit a fragile one—which resulted in the contested territory becoming a Marcher lordship of two parts—an Englishry and a Welshry.

Domination—the Castle

The above sequence of events may have taken place in Gower; if it did, then the early stages must have occurred between 1106 and 1116, for an entry in the *Peniarth MS 20* version of the *Brut* relating to 1116 records a Welsh attack on 'a castle which Earl Henry,

The slopes of the knoll on which Beaumont established his castle are still discernable in Swansea's city centre. The photograph shows the steep slope to the Strand and the remains of a later stone-walled castle.

who was called Beaumont, had at Abertawe'. The castle is believed to have been built on a knoll in Swansea City Centre, the most defensible site in the locality. Although much of the knoll is now masked by 20th-century buildings, evidence of its extent is still discernible. On the east, Welcome Lane and the slope above the Strand provide a glimpse of a scarp that would have deterred any attacker. At the southern end of the knoll the fall is not so steep, but it is still evident in Castle Lane and Castle Square (between the remains of the later castle of *c.*1300 that can be seen today and Castle Gardens). On the west, what used to be a steep slope is now hidden by David Evan's store, although the paved walkway between the store and Castle Gardens highlights the difference in elevation between Castle Street and Princess Way. On the north, at the junction between High Street and Castle Street, the rise is slight, but still noticeable.

The *Red Book of Hergest* version of the attack in 1116 states that the Welsh withdrew 'after burning the outer castle'. There is no indisputable trace of Beaumont's 'outer castle', but it can be confidently assumed that it occupied the same area—namely the knoll—as the later stone-walled 'outer bailey' that is referred to in documents relating to the late 13th century. The ditch of the later 'outer bailey' surrounded the knoll on three sides, and sections of it have been found in Welcome Lane, College Street, Castle Gardens and beneath David Evan's store—in short, it is where it should be, on the low ground surrounding the knoll, except on the east where the steep fall to the Strand provided adequate protection on that side. It follows that Beaumont's ditch must surely have been sited in exactly the same place. The fact that no 12th-century material has been found in the ditch may be due to periodic clearances to prevent it silting up (see p.112).

A palisade probably encompassed the fairly level summit of the knoll on all four sides; moreover, the stone wall which replaced it is known to have enclosed an area of 4.3 acres, almost as large as the five-acre interior of the Roman fort at Loughor. If Beaumont's 'outer castle' had also been 4.3 acres, then its garrison must have been considerable, although it would have varied according to the military situation at any given time. A charter of *c.*1170 refers to the presence of men-at-arms at Swansea without stating their number, but Gerald mentioned that, about this time, the garrison at Cardiff consisted of 120 men-at-arms (the figure probably included retainers) and a numerous body of archers, which suggests a garrison several hundred strong. The garrison at Swansea may not have been so numerous, but in 1116 it must have been of sufficient strength to keep the natives in check; it may even have been employed in terrorizing the natives into submission.

Reference to an 'outer castle' implies there had been an inner one as well, and the *Hergest* version of the attack records that, 'after burning the outer castle, and the keepers had saved the tower', the Welsh withdrew. Reference to a tower has prompted many to classify Beaumont's 'inner castle' as a motte—a pudding-shaped mound—the summit of which would have carried a wooden 'tower'. There can be no doubt that the 'inner castle' was sited to the north of the ruinous castle that can be seen today, that being the highest and most defensible part of the knoll.

In 1913, when excavations for town improvements were carried out in the area between Castle Street and Worcester Place, Colonel W. Ll. Morgan, a local historian, made notes of what the workmen uncovered. The following year he wrote *The Castle of Swansea* in which he presented a case for locating Beaumont's 'inner castle' immediately to the north of what used to be the Castle Cinema. About 30m. south of Welcome Lane a watercourse ran eastwards, according to Morgan, from Worcester Place to the Strand; another watercourse ran southwards, between Worcester Place and Castle Street, then turned eastwards down Castle Lane, again to the Strand. When the Anglo-Normans occupied the knoll they enlarged sections of the watercourses to create a ditch, piling the spoil immediately to the north of the Castle Cinema site to form the motte. The ditch was no doubt extended to encircle the motte on three sides, but not on the east due of the steep fall to the Strand.

At a later date, possibly in the late 12th or early 13th century, the motte was levelled, according to Morgan, and the spoil used to fill in the ditch. A new ditch was then dug to enclose a stone-walled castle on the same site. Morgan's findings, however, have recently been challenged by another local historian who has argued that Beaumont's 'inner castle' had not been a motte surmounted by a 'tower', but a ring-work—a level, circular area with a raised lip around the perimeter that carried a palisade. The lip and the palisade were then replaced by the curtain wall of the later stone castle, the remains of which were unearthed in the 1913 excavations.

Lordship of Gower

If the knoll was in Anglo-Norman hands by 1116, then the southern sub-commote of *Is-coed* must also have been in their hands by *c.*1119, the year in which Beaumont is believed to have granted four churches in the Peninsula to the Abbey of St. Taurin of Evreux in Normandy. It is these two issues—the castle and the grant of four churches—that establishes Beaumont as the first Anglo-Norman lord of Gower; moreover, his seizure of land in Wales made him a Marcher lord, meaning that within his Lordship of Gower he assumed to himself the role and privileges of a Welsh king and that he—or at least his officers—had authority to try people for serious offences which, in England, could only be dealt with by the Crown.

The Anglo-Norman Settlement

It appears that several men-at-arms and possibly two Marcher lords acquired estates—variously termed fiefs, fees, manors or mesne lordships—that established them as a new landholding warrior aristocracy in certain parts of Gower. Later sources suggest that these men, known as mesne lords, acquired more than one fief, each of which would have provided sufficient means for a man-at-arms to furnish his own horses, arms and equipment. These mesne lords, as a result of their acquisitions, became Beaumont's vassals, holding each of their fiefs on the condition that they served Beaumont in a military capacity at their own expense for a period of at least 40 days each year. Usually, this meant performing a minimum of 40 days castle guard at Swansea where they devoted time to training—an essential requirement as these mesne lords and their descendants were to find themselves 'living in a constant state of warfare'.

It is not possible to identify the fiefs created as a result of Beaumont's conquest, nor the mesne lords who were first possessed of them, although most of the mesne lords would, no doubt, have had French names, the second names usually preceded by *fitz*, meaning 'son of', or by *de*, meaning 'of' or 'from' the place where they or their forefathers originated. By the early 12th century, second names such as fitzBaldwin and de Newburgh had become family names, although nicknames such as William *Rufus*, meaning William with the red hair, were still in vogue.

In any attempt to identify fiefs that existed in the 12th century it has been common for historians to refer to a charter of 1306, which lists the names of 12 'old knights' fees' that allegedly date to the reign of Henry I (1100-35). The list, however, is both incomplete and inaccurate. Kilvrough, for example, was certainly a fief in 1306,

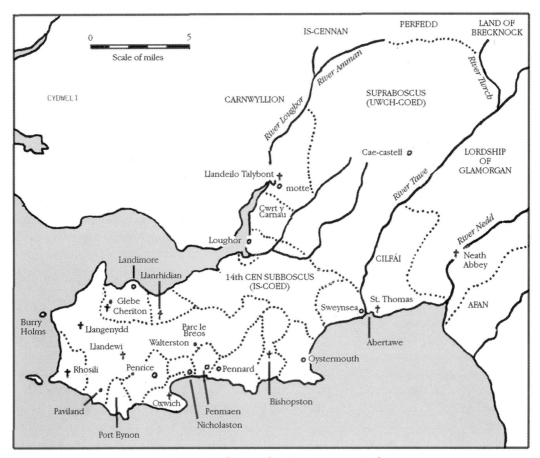

Gower in the Anglo-Norman period.

but it does not appear in the list, whereas Weobley, which is listed, was not created a fief until 1304. A more reliable, though apparently incomplete, list appears in the 1166 returns of Earl William (Beaumont's grandson), which records the names of three of his vassals in Gower—William de Turberville, Terricus Hareng and Lucas.

William de Turberville was Lord of Landimore, which comprised of three fiefs—Rhosili, Llanrhidian, and Landimore proper (the parish of Cheriton and the later fief of Weobley mentioned above). His title is established by a confirmatory charter, which records that he granted the churches of Rhosili, Landimore (Cheriton) and Llanrhidian to the Order of Knights Hospitaller. He was undoubtedly a descendant of the Marcher lord, Payn de Turberville, who may have been one of the mesne lords enfeoffed as a result Beaumont's conquest. Payn appears to have had a presence in Gower because, in 1131, the Bishop of Llandaff complained to the Pope that 'Rabel, chamberlain of Turberville', had 'violently ejected him from' Bishopston. Terricus Hareng was the ancestor of Philip Hareng who, in 1241, recovered the fief of Penmaen on the instructions of Henry III. Lucas cannot be linked with any particular fief, nor can it be assumed that he was an ancestor of the notorious Lucas family of the Early Modern period.

In conclusion the 1166 returns are not that informative, but information on early fiefs can be gleaned from other sources, such as confirmatory charters. Whenever a landowner gifted land to a religious institution it was common practice to enter the relevant details in a charter that could be referred to whenever there was a dispute. All the original 12th-century charters relevant to Gower are no longer in existence, but the details of some have survived in what are known as confirmatory charters. Neath Abbey, for instance, received numerous gifts of land following its foundation in 1130; sometime after 1176 the monks took the precaution of recording the relevant details of these donations in one document and then had Bishop Leia of St. David's (1176-98) put his name to it. The original 12th-century charters that had been presented to Neath Abbey have all been lost, but the confirmatory charter of Bishop Leia survived to bear witness to the grants.

One entry in Leia's confirmatory charter reads:

> in the land which Geoffrey Panchefot held the fief of Llandeilo Talybont, which falls between the waters of the Lliw and Loughor and between the streams which fall into the Loughor, which Henry de Vilers gave to the monks in alms, with the consent of Henry de Warwick; the Chapel of St. Michael, with the land and pastures and other easements, which they have of Henry de Vilers.

What this entry records is that Henry de Vilers originally held the fief of Llandeilo Talybont, and that he subsequently enfeoffed Geoffrey Panchefot in the fief, thereby making Panchefot his vassal. At a later date de Vilers granted a parcel of wasteland in the southern part of the fief of Llandeilo Talybont to Neath Abbey, and did so with the consent of Henry de Warwick who, as a younger son of Beaumont, appears to have had control of Gower between *c.*1138 and *post*-1166. The donation became the grange of Cwrt y Carnau; the Chapel of St. Michael was founded to serve the needs of the brethren who administered the grange.

It has been accepted—though not proved—that Henry de Vilers also held the fief of Loughor, but by c. 1165 Loughor was in the hands Henry de Warwick, the man who gave his consent to the donation. Loughor seems to have remained in the possession of the lords of Gower until it passed to John Iweyn during the reign of Edward I (1272-1307), by which time Llandeilo Talybont also belonged to the lords of Gower. As to the de Vilers family, the last recorded member was Sir John de Vilers who witnessed a charter of 1320. That John held the title of 'sir', coupled with the fact that his place among the witnesses is second only to that of Sir Robert Penres, suggests that he was an important landowner, but his fiefs are entirely unknown.

Another charter, dated to 1141, records that Maurice de Londres made a gift of Oystermouth Church (with its tithes) to St. Peter's Abbey, Gloucester. This suggests that Maurice held the parish of Oystermouth as a fief; he may even have inherited the fief from his father, William, for the *Brut* records that, in 1116, the Welsh insurgents under Gruffudd ap Rhys attacked not only Beaumont's castle at Abertawe, but another (unnamed) castle as well. The relevant entry states: 'A castle that was in Gower he [Gruffudd ap Rhys] burnt outright and slew many within it. William de Londres, through fear, left the castle that was in his charge'. The two sentences, together with Maurice's charter, have led historians to believe that the unnamed castle was Oystermouth, though this is by no means certain. The de Londres family may have held other fiefs in Gower—West Pilton among them—but by 1284 Oystermouth had ceased to be a fief and had become a demesne, the personal property of the lords of Gower.

Other fiefs no doubt existed in 12th-century Gower, but only Penres, which, at that time, probably included the later sub-fief of Horton, need be considered here. Bishop Leia's confirmatory charter to the Hospitallers mentions: 'the gift of Robert de Penres, the Church of St. Andrew of Penres'. The name Penres (better known today as Penrice) is a corruption of Penrhys, a Welsh name meaning 'the head of Rhys', though that does not mean the founder of the family was Welsh. He may have adopted the name of the locality, which raises the possibility that the earliest fiefs were originally Welsh *trefi* (see p.56), each with a tenancy paying dues and a church dedicated to a Welsh saint.

Anglo-Norman Seizure of Church Property

A papal bull, dated 16 October 1119, was issued by Pope Calixtus II who decreed, in support of Urban, Bishop of Llandaff, 'that it shall not be lawful for any man whatsoever to rashly disturb the aforesaid church [of Llandaff] or take away its possessions'. That same day the Pope wrote to the barons of south-east Wales, commanding them 'to restore without delay the land, tithes, oblations and sepultures' that belonged to Llandaff. The Pope listed in his bull the properties that had been 'taken away', six of which were in Gower—St. Teilo de Llanferwallt, Llancynwalan, Llandeilo Porthtulon, Llandeilo Talybont, Llangemei and Cilcynhin. Two of these properties, Llandeilo

Porthtulon and Cilcynhin, cannot be located and, therefore, nothing can be said of them except that they were mentioned in 6th and 7th century charters, but the seizure of the remaining four properties provides insight into the Anglo-Norman intrusion into Gower.

The bounds of Llandeilo Talybont enclosed land on both sides of the Loughor, and in several bulls the property is referred to as a *vill*, which the Welsh would have regarded as an ecclesiastical *tref*, one in which there was a church (not a monastery) dedicated to St. Teilo, and one in which Welsh tenants paid their dues to the bishops of Llandaff. The details surrounding the seizure of this property are obscure, but by the time of Henry de Warwick (*c.*1138 to *post*-1166) that part of the *tref* on the east bank of the River Loughor had become the fief of Llandeilo Talybont, its bounds coinciding with the present-day parish bearing the same name. The Llancynwalan property is synonymous with the 7th-century 'cell of Cynwalan with all its land', the bounds of which appear to enclose the western half of the parish of Rhosili (less the later, eastern additions of Pitton and Pilton); if this is correct, then Llancynwalan became the fief of Rhosili, which William de Turberville held in 1166 as part of his dispersed estate of Landimore.

The fate of Llangemei (Llangenydd) is revealed by an entry in a confirmatory charter of 1195 to the monks of St. Taurin of Evreux in Normandy. The entry, which records a gift of Henry Beaumont, reads:

> Henry, Earl of Warwick, who, for the souls of his Lord King William [Rufus] and Queen Matilda, and to himself, gave in Wales the Church of Kenetus [St. Cenydd], and land for two ploughs in the vicinity of the church, and the tithes of the vill, a suitable spot for the mill, and enough of his woods for all the needs of the brethren, and a tithe of the rents there, and his hunting and fishing and all his demesne; and the Church of St. Taurin and Penart with their tithes and the Church of the Isle [Burry Holms] free of all claims.

The grant brought French-speaking, black-robed, Benedictine monks to what later became known as Prior's Town (the eastern end of the village of Llangenydd), where they established a priory at what is now College Farm on the southern side of the church. Most documents relating to this cell suggest that it was occupied by a prior and a companion monk. The monks were responsible for managing what was really a small manor, and no doubt collected the tithes that were due to the 'Church of St. Taurin [possibly Knelston] and Penart [Pennard]', as well as the 'tithes of the vill'—the vill of Llangenydd, that is, which Beaumont otherwise retained for himself.

The last property to be considered is St. Teilo de Llanferwallt, described in a bull of 1131 as 'the vill of St. Teilo de Lannuallt'. Despite the bull of 1119, this property (along with those mentioned above) had not been returned to Llandaff by 1128, the year in which a second pope issued a bull which listed the same six Gower properties. Then, in 1131, a third pope issued yet another bull in response to Bishop Urban's complaint that 'Rabel, chamberlain of Turberville, had violently ejected him from ... the vill of St. Teilo de Lannualt'. The matter was resolved in 1133 when Urban was confirmed in his possession of Llanferwallt, although later lords of Gower frequently laid claim to what was really a separate lordship within the Lordship of Gower, one in which the tenants were subject to the jurisdiction of Llandaff.

Mention has already been made of C.A. Seyler's claim that the bounds of Bishopston parish more or less correspond to those given for the Church of Cyngur Trosgardi in the charter of Morgan ab Arthrwys. This claim, however, does not tie in with 17th- and 18th-century surveys which make it plain that the bishop's lordship comprised of only the southern half of the parish, a thoroughly Anglicized area in which the soil was ideally suited for manorial cultivation. The less fertile northern half of the parish—between Broadly Water and Upper Killay—continued to be occupied by free Welshmen; moreover, by the early 15th century it becomes evident that the northern half of the parish was a detached part of Weobley, a fief that in 1304 had been carved out of Landimore proper, once a possession of the de Turberville family. It is possible, therefore, that prior to 1119 the man responsible for 'taking away' the bishop's property of St. Teilo de Llanferwallt (and Llancynwalan) was none other than the Marcher lord, Payn de Turberville, and that, owing to papal pressure, he subsequently returned only the southern half of 'the vill of Lannuallt' to the Bishop of Llandaff.

The bull of 1119 establishes that *Is-coed* was definitely in Anglo-Norman hands by that date; it also suggests that Beaumont's followers had rights of seizure, which they presumed to include ecclesiastical *trefi* and, with the exception of Llanferwallt, were not swayed by papal threats to return several named *trefi* to Llandaff. It, therefore, follows that Beaumont's followers would have had no qualms about seizing secular *trefi*, especially if they had overwhelmed or killed a native ruler. The advantage of seizing *trefi* as opposed to undefined territory was that the *trefi* were territorial units in which land tenure, obligations and dues were well established. A sudden change in ownership—from, say, a bishop to a mesne lord—need not have brought a halt to the rhythm of land. The same can be said of secular *trefi*, the tenants of which had, until the intrusion, paid their dues to Welsh rulers. This hypotheses would explain why almost all the earliest known fiefs have names that are Welsh, or derived from Welsh, *viz.* Llandeilo Talybont, Loughor, Llanrhidian, Landimore, Rhosili, Port Eynon, Penres, Penmaen and also the lord's demesne of Pennard; even the name of Oystermouth may derive from its Welsh counterpart, Ystum llymarch, meaning 'Oyster bend'.

Subsidiary Castles

The Anglo-Normans built between eight and thirteen subsidiary castles, most of them ring-works, a few promontory and one motte. Two were sited at fords on the River Loughor to guard against incursions from the west; the remainder were in the Peninsula. With the exception of Pennard—which belonged to Beaumont—they were

The raised ring-work at Loughor.
The stone ruins on the right are the remains of a later stone gate-tower.

The motte of Castle Du, Llandeilo Talybont.

probably the fortified residences of mesne lords. Little that is visible remains at most sites; some have been all but ploughed out over the centuries, others are concealed by dense vegetation. Two—Oystermouth and Pennard—were rebuilt in stone, leaving little or no trace of earlier banks and ditches. Loughor, which commanded the ford over the Loughor Estuary, was also rebuilt in stone, but its raised platform remains a good example of what a ring-work looked like, more so if one imagines, around the rim of the platform, a raised lip carrying a palisade of pointed stakes. A ditch may have protected the ring-work on the north and west.

The remains of a motte can be seen from the M4 motorway by motorists travelling westwards towards junction 48. Eighty years ago this motte stood 9m. tall, its summit originally crowned by a wooden tower. Known by a variety of names, the most frequently used being Castle Du, this early castle not only overlooked a ford on the River Loughor, but it was home to the mesne lords of Llandeilo Talybont. To the south, traces of a bank and ditch mark the position of a bailey.

It is unfortunate that Penrice Old Castle, otherwise known as Mounty Brough, is overgrown and on private land because it is another fine example of a ring-work castle. As with all early ring-works a wooden gate-tower no doubt dominated the entrance on the north, its upper floor serving as living quarters and as a place where archers could shoot at attackers from narrow windows. The remains of a ditch exist on the west; the bailey probably extended eastwards towards the Church of St. Andrew.

Domestic Buildings

The remains of halls have been found at two castles—Pennard and Penmaen—and the remnants of an undefended hall were found beneath sand on the warren to the west of Rhosili Down. In all three cases low, dry-stone walls have preserved the outline of rectangular buildings with rounded corners. The hall within Pennard Castle proved to be 18.6m. long by 7.6m. wide, divided internally into a private chamber, the hall itself and two small service rooms; the door faced east, towards the main gate.

Near Cheriton Church is Glebe Farm which, dating from the late 13th century, is the oldest occupied building in Gower. It is classified as a three-unit hall-house, the units ranged around an oblong courtyard. For most of its existence Glebe Farm has served as a rectory. Yet the size of its hall, which originally occupied the whole of the eastern unit and lay open to the rafters, and also the solar (private quarters) on the first floor of the southern unit, suggest that it had originally been built to be something more than the home of a clergyman. It is possibly the work of the Hospitallers who, in c.1165, had been granted the Church of Landimore/Cheriton, or maybe it was the home of a well-to-do landowner, even a mesne lord.

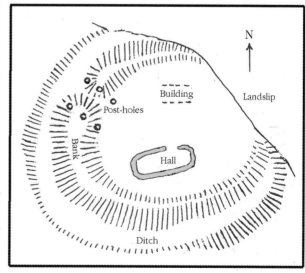

Castle Tower, Penmaen.

Glebe Farm, built in the late 13th century; the oldest occupied building in Gower.

English Settlers

Some mesne lords encouraged English settlement in their fiefs to the extent that Isaac Hamon wrote, in 1696-7, that the people on 'the south side of Gower did pronounce their words something like the West of England'. Initially, English settlement may have been concentrated in the fiefs/parishes of Port Eynon, Oxwich, Penres, Nicholaston, Penmaen and in the lord's demesne/parish of Pennard, where 16th- to 18th-century surveys make it plain that the measurement of land was based on a nine-foot pole, a measurement that originated in the West of England. Elsewhere in west and south Gower, English settlement appears to have been less intense and, in some areas, may have taken place at a later date. Almost nothing is known about these people until the 14th century, after which it becomes increasingly clear, especially from the 16th century onwards, that the majority were customary tenants—also known as *coloni* (farmers) and *villeins* (feudal tenants) — whose status differed little from Welsh *taeogion*.

For a share in the open fields common to the fief (or manor) where they were settled, customary tenants were obliged to work the mesne lord's fields, ploughing, harvesting and carrying out other forms of manual labour, in return for which they received the mesne lord's protection. They were also obliged to pay, in money or in kind, a low, annual rent for every acre that was allocated to them; on top of which they had to pay fines (taxes) for basic requirements such as grinding their corn in the mesne lord's mill, something they were compelled to do. If any of them were involved in a dispute, or indicted for a minor offence, their pleas were heard in the mesne lord's manorial court to which their fellow tenants were obliged to do suit, meaning they were expected to attend as jurors.

The remains of a tenant's croft of late 12th to early 13th-century date have been found beneath sand near Pennard Castle. The shape of the croft was that of an unsymmetrical oblong, 5m. by 3m., with rounded corners. A layer of soot and charcoal—probably the remains of a thatched roof—covered a red, clay floor, showing that the croft had been burnt, the daub walls collapsing on top of the debris. Finds included pottery, a spindle-whorl, a fragment of a bone knife handle and a barbed and socketed arrowhead. The croft was undoubtedly one of several that now lie buried beneath sand, for it was recorded in 1291 that 'a few wooden buildings nearby [the castle] completed the villa de Penarth'.

Evidence of open fields can still be found in the parishes of Rhosili and Bishopston. In Rhosili the fields were known collectively as the Vile, or Great Field, which lies to the south of the present-day parish church, enclosed by a dry-stone wall. Originally, most of the fields within the Vile were long, narrow strips separated by baulks that have since been removed or superseded by quite high banks. Some fields were no doubt assigned to the mesne lord while others were allocated to the tenants. Crop rotation would have resulted in many fields being left fallow to be grazed by livestock, their dung fertilizing the soil.

No surveys of fiefs have survived from the Anglo-Norman period, but the *Black Book of St. David's* records a survey of the bishop of St. David's tiny manor of Llandewi, which comprised only a small portion of the modern-day parish of the same name. This survey—or extent—which was carried out in 1326, provides a glimpse of the manorial set-up that must have existed on the south side of the Peninsula at that time. The survey records: 'as to the bishop's demesne there were, by counting quarries and other stony places, 124 acres of land; each acre worth yearly to let 12d.' It was accepted that, on the arable land, 'there ought to be sown' wheat, beans, barley, great and small oats, 'which the bishop was able to plough with one plough, and on the rest to keep 8 oxen [and] 120 sheep'. There appears to have been three customary tenants residing in the manor—William Gammon, John Gammon and Adam Ryng—each of whom paid rent for the acreage they held, which ranged from 3/4 to 2 acres. All three tenants, on succeeding to their father's possessions, had been obliged to give the bishop 'for a heriot' (a form of death duty) their 'best beast, or if they had no beast 5s.'. William and John Gammon were obliged 'to reap for two days [a year on the bishop's land], the bishop providing food. The same two were to plough for two days, the bishop providing food'. All three 'did suit' in the bishop's manorial court.

Three men—Robert Canan, Elys Rowe and William Camman—were empanelled as jurors; they provided the information contained in the survey. It is generally assumed they were free men, although they are not described as such, nor is there reference to them paying dues. There is also the possibility that 'William Camman' is a misspelling of William Gammon, the name of a customary tenant mentioned above. On the basis of the six names mentioned in the survey it has been assumed that only six men resided in the manor. The assumption may, however, be flawed as the survey was not intended to list all the tenants, but to record the bishop's income, including profits from building stone, wood and a garden, which contained 'fruit and feeding' to the value of 3s. As a result of the evidence provided by the jurors the value of the manor was reckoned to be 36s. yearly.

Similar conditions to those recorded at Llandewi would have existed within the fiefs that ranged along the fertile 'south side' of the Peninsula, although everything within these fiefs would have been on a much larger scale. Each fief would have had a church (the one at Llandewi was not mentioned in the survey as tithes were due to the Church, not the bishop), a mill and the mesne lord's residence, be it a hall or a subsidiary castle. There is no mention of an overseer at Llandewi, but the management of a fief would have been in the hands of a steward or bailiff. A fief would also have contained a number of free Anglo-Norman/English landowners whose status was below that of the mesne lord.

The Lord's Demesne
The present-day parish of Pennard was definitely in Beaumont's possession as a demesne manor by 1119, the year in which he is believed to have granted the 'Church of Penart' to an abbey in Normandy. The manor is an oddity in that it bears the hallmarks of an early fief: it was Anglicized and had a castle—an early ring-work—on the same site as the ruinous stone castle that can be seen today. Pennard may have been held by a mesne lord who died childless shortly after the Anglo-Norman intrusion, in which case it would have escheated to Beaumont. It remained in the possession of Beaumont's successors until the northern half became the fiefs of Kilvrough and Kittle, the former possibly in the late 13th century. Loughor—which may also have been an early fief—was a demesne manor by c.1156. Other fiefs were to escheat to the lords of Gower at unrecorded dates, but none were to compare with the most important demesne manor of all.

The Town and Manor of Swansea
The town, or borough, of Swansea took root outside the walls of the 'castle that Beaumont ... had at Abertawe'. The earliest reference to the borough's existence comes from a hoard of coins found at Cardiff, nine or ten of which bore a variety of inscriptions such as *Sven, Svenshi* and *Swensi*. The earliest of the nine or ten coins also bear the name of (King) Stephen, but from 1141 onwards the name was replaced by *Henrici de Noveb*—Henry de Newburgh, alias de Warwick, Beaumont's son and heir to the Lordship of Gower. Henry came to Gower in c.1138, shortly before a civil war in England caused a shortage of coinage. In all probability Henry minted the coins

to facilitate paying both the Swansea garrison and the civilians who catered for the garrison's needs—butchers, bakers, brewers and the like.

The castle, moreover, was ideally situated to attract merchants. Prior to the mid-19th century, when the lower Tawe was diverted to its present position further east (now the New Cut), the river flowed close to the Strand, its course curving westwards from below High Street Station to where Sainsbury's supermarket stands today, at which point it flowed into what was known in the 19th century as Fabian's Bay, now occupied by the docks to the east of Sainsbury's store. Merchants could, therefore, offload their cargoes of cloth, wine, corn, salt and pottery close to the castle, and buy in exchange skins, hides and wool that came from the surrounding countryside.

The evidence of the coins is supported by a confirmatory charter of Bishop Anselm to the Hospitallers, dated 1230, which records 'the gift of Henry de Newburgh, the Church of Lochor [Loughor] ... and in the vill of the same name one burgage, with another burgage in the vill of Sweynsea [Swansea]'. So there were two boroughs in Gower during the time of Henry de Newburgh, both of them providing him with an additional source of income in the form of taxes and amercements.

As an incentive for craftsmen and merchants to settle in the lordship, Henry (and possibly his father before him) offered each and every entrepreneur a burgage—a plot of land in one or other of the boroughs for an annual rent of 12 pence on which to build a 'house, oven, brewhouse', and no doubt other buildings as well. Those who took up the offer became burgesses—privileged, often wealthy citizens who were not bound to their burgages by military or customary obligations, but were free to practise a craft or travel in pursuit of trade. The burgesses also had the right to limited self-government, although the only officer-bearer mentioned in a charter of c.1170 was the 'toll-collector', who appears to have been responsible for the collection of any money due to the lord or to the borough funds. In a deed of c.1200 one Adam Croyland is styled 'preposito ville de Sweynes', which makes him the earliest known chief officer of the borough. In later centuries the chief officer became known as the *portreeve*, whose election to office was yearly at Michaelmas (29 September).

The earliest description of a town house is in a document dated 1400, which records the assignment of a third of *Sweynsea* and Gower to the then Duchess of Norfolk as her dower; the description reads: 'two cellars near the [southern] bridge of the bailey, four shops above the said cellars, two chambers built above the aforesaid shops'. The chambers were where the burgesses met to discuss the affairs of the borough. The house was situated inside the 'outer bailey', against the south wall, in the south-eastern corner of what is now Castle Gardens.

Little is known of the borough of Loughor other than that is was probably quite small, its burgesses numbering little more than a dozen, whereas *Sweynsea* had more than 63 burgesses in 1400, possibly more than 100. *Sweynsea* also has a better recorded history, one of its more informative treasures being a charter of c.1170, granted by Beaumont's grandson, William de Newburgh, Earl of Warwick. This

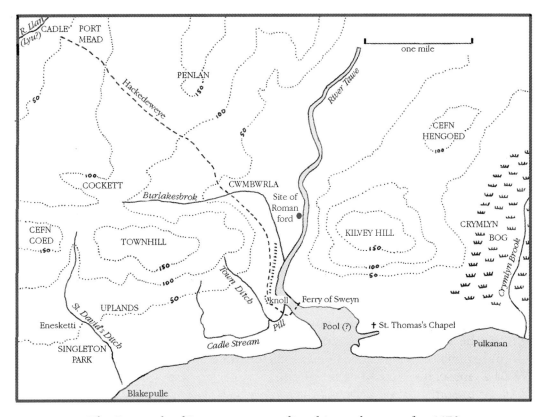

The Borough of Sweynsea *as outlined in a charter of* c. 1170.

charter provides a comprehensive account of the privileges of the *Sweynsea* burgesses, whose sphere of influence extended far beyond the town. The borough, or manor, of *Sweynsea* contained almost 2,000 acres, bounded on the south by the sea, on the west by *St. David's Ditch* (the Brynmill Stream as far as Cefn Coed), on the north and north-west by *Burlakesbrok* (the Burlais Brook, which rose near Cockett Station to flow down through Cwmbwrla and join the Tawe just below High Street Station). The Tawe formed the eastern boundary as far as the sea.

The charter of *c.*1170 makes it plain that the burgesses were farmers as well as entrepreneurs, each of them having rights 'to seven acres beyond the woods [which surrounded the borough] and above Burlakesbrok, and pasture as far as Hackedeweye [Pentregethin Road], and as far as Lyu [probably the River Llan], and as far as St. David's Ditch'. Earl William also granted them rights to 'the woods on all sides of [his] borough to pasture their herds, [feed] their pigs [and] take oak to make their houses, fences and ships, rendering for a ship twelve pence, and all other wood for their fire[s]'. They were free to hunt 'without hindrance all the wild beasts [in his] wood ... except the stag, the hind, the wild boar and the marten'. He granted them rights to 'fisheries [which presumably involved erecting stake-nets] between

Pulkanan [Pwllcynon] and Blakepulle [Black Pill]', the only proviso being that all 'porpoise and sturgeon' belonged to him.

In another clause William stipulated that should the burgesses 'find wreck outside the pool [possibly Fabian's Bay] when the tide ebbs, it may be half mine and half theirs. And if they find wreck on dry land it shall be all mine'. As to their activities beyond farming, fishing and catering for the garrison's needs, some of the burgesses were engaged in ship-building, while others were involved in either the cloth or leather trade, for it states in the charter that 'no foreign merchant may cut cloths by retail, nor buy skins or hides, except from a burgess'. The burgesses had, in fact, a monopoly on all trade; this is made clear in a charter of 1306, which confirms the burgesses' expectations 'that no outside merchant shall trade in merchandize within our borough of Sweyn, or in the land of Gower, except the burgesses of Loughor'.

Although they did not hold their burgages by military tenure, the burgesses were nevertheless expected to take up arms in response to any threat by Welsh insurgents, for William stipulated that if he (or more likely his officers) 'shall summon my burgesses to the army, or to any affair of mine, they shall go at their expense if it so be that they can return to their homes the same night. And if I shall lead them further away, they shall be at my expense'. It is clear from these entries that military expeditions involving the burgesses were, for the most part, limited to sallies into the surrounding countryside.

It is likely that the charter was granted because the burgesses had complained that their rights had been abused by either William's officers, or by his predecessor, Henry de Warwick (d. post-1166). Evidence in support of this supposition may be gleaned from entries in the charter relating to the burgesses' judicial privileges, which state that 'if a burgess shall make a forfeiture [commit a crime], and shall be brought into my court [at *Sweynsea* Castle] by view of his neighbours and not have pledges [material things given as security], or sureties [persons willing to take responsibility for him], then he shall plead [his cause] in my court. And if he shall have bail by pledges and sureties, he shall plead in his hundred court', held at one time in the town house mentioned above, where he was be tried and punished by his fellow burgesses.

There were several other clauses to suggest previous abuses, the most notable being that 'it is not allowed for any of my household to bear witness against a burgess'. Another grievance that may have had something to do with garrison troops is suggested by the stipulation that 'whoever shall shed blood from noon on Saturday to Monday morning, [shall be fined] forty shillings in forfeit. And from Monday morning to noon Saturday, twelve pence in forfeit, except for premeditated assault and forestallage'. Weekend brawls were obviously as much a problem then as they are now.

As to the earliest burgesses on record, a late 12th-century list of the burgesses of Dublin provides the names of two merchants who were also burgesses of

Sweynsea, both of whom appear to have had Norse names—Godafridus and Ricardus filius (son of) Segeri. It is likely that these two merchants were originally *Sweynsea* burgesses who acquired duel citizenship to take advantage of the trading opportunities that were to result from King Henry II's charter of 1172 to the burgesses of Dublin. Bishop Anselm's charter to the Hospitallers provides the name of another *Sweynsea* burgess when it refers to 'the burgage of William, son of the Palmer'. William may have been an Anglo-Norman; his father, the Palmer, would have been a pilgrim who had returned from the Holy Land with a palm branch in his possession. The same charter mentions the 'gift of John de Penres, the house [presumed to have been in Sweynsea] of the Hospitallers which he built for charitable use'. It is reasonable to assume that John was Lord of Penres; if so, it would not have been unusual for him to be a burgess as well. Later evidence shows that many mesne lords held one or more burgages in *Sweynsea*, for not only did the ownership of a burgage provide opportunities for investment, but mesne lords kept huge flocks of sheep to meet the growing demands of the wool merchants. The sum of these snippets of information is that Scandinavians and Anglo-Normans were definitely present in 12th-century *Sweynsea*; there may even have been English and Flemings there too, but the one people who would not have been allowed to own a burgage at that time were the Welsh.

The Englishry

Fiefs, the lord's demesne and two boroughs all formed part of the Englishry of Gower—known in Latin text as *Anglicana*—where English language, law and customs prevailed. There were, of course, other languages in use besides English. Norman-French was the language of the nobility, the lawcourts and the church hierarchy, continuing as such until the 14th century. Latin would have been heard at Mass and was the language used in charters. Welsh probably persisted within the Englishry, though to what extent is difficult to determine. A little Norse and perhaps Flemish may have been spoken in the towns.

The earliest evidence of English law in Gower is to be found in that part of Earl William's charter that deals with the burgesses' privilege to be judged and sentenced by their peers. The charter also refers to Earl William's (county) court—the highest in Gower—which, according to a charter of 1306, dealt with serious offences such as murder, theft and arson. An entry in the *Breviate of Domesday* for the year 1287 mentions 'the law of twelve and of inquest'; what this meant becomes clear in the charter of 1306 to 'the English and Welsh of the English County of Gower'—the County being the Englishry which, by 1306, had expanded to include almost the whole of the Peninsula as well as the manors of *Sweynsea*, Loughor and Llandeilo Talybont. The charter does not mention 'inquest'—to ascertain the facts—but it does confirm the role of the mesne lords in the County Court, and the list of 12 'old knights' fees' may be representative of the number of jurors required. There were certainly more that 12 mesne lords in Gower at that time, all of whom had an obligation to 'do suit' at the County Court, where they served as jurors, assembling 'monthly on Monday' according to Merrick. Most non-capital offences were punishable by amercements (fines), a profitable source of income for the lords of Gower.

As to customs, one of the most noteworthy differences between the newcomers and the native Welsh was in respect of inheritance. Among the Anglo-Norman aristocracy it was the norm for estates to be held 'in tail' and to pass undivided to the eldest surviving son providing that he had reached the age of 21. There were, however, occasions in which a younger son might be given a small portion of the family estate. For example, when Beaumont died the bulk of his estate passed to his eldest son, Roger de Newburgh, whereas a younger son, Henry de Newburgh, became 'heir to' Gower. A similar arrangement may have taken place among the de Turbervilles (whose main seat was at Coety) as their Landimore fiefs were, in 1166, in the hands of William de Turberville, a member of a cadet branch of the family. Succession among customary tenants varied. In the manor of Bishopston, for example, their lands descended by 'borough English', meaning they passed undivided to the youngest son.

The Welsh within the Englishry

It may be presumed that in the fief of Llandeilo Talybont, where manorial cultivation was not viable and where Welsh place-names still dominate the landscape, the Welsh remained the dominant element. The same assumption holds true for the fiefs/manors on the 'north side' of the Peninsula as several early 14th-century charters testify to the existence of Welsh tenants and the survival of Welsh place-names in the fiefs/manors of Llangenydd, Landimore proper and Llanrhidian. However, the same charters show that English free men were making inroads into these areas, gradually Anglicizing them to the extent that, in 1696-7, Isaac Hamon claimed the people on 'the north side' of the Peninsula were 'inclined more to the Welsh, and mixed some Welsh words amongst their old English'. By the 18th century this part of the 'north side' had become thoroughly Anglicized.

On the 'south side' where the land was fertile and, therefore, ideally suited to manorial cultivation, it is difficult to determine what happened to the Welsh who, prior to the Anglo-Norman intrusion, had been living within a mile or so of the sea. Apart from the names of fiefs and a few dedications to Welsh saints, the place-names with any historical significance on the 'south side' are almost entirely of English origin, evidence that suggests the Welsh were displaced. It may, however, be reasonable to assume that the Anglo-Normans found it expedient to have Welsh *taeogion*—who were already tied to the land—work alongside English customary tenants. Free Welshmen, had they also been allowed to remain in the Englishry, may have been deprived of their best lands, but the fact that their holdings were scattered may have limited their losses, even though the lands they retained were situated in less fertile parts. Hypotheses such as these would explain why churches at Port Eynon, Oxwich and Bishopston have retained their dedications to Welsh saints.

The Welshry—the *Wallicana* of the Latin Text.

Beyond the Anglo-Norman dominated areas lay the less fertile lands of the Welshry, which consisted of three administrative areas—*Is-coed, Uwch-coed* and *Cilfái* (Kilvey). The sub-commote of *Is-coed*—better known by its Latin equivalent of *Subboscus*—comprised of what remained of the coastal lowlands after the Anglo-Normans had created fiefs, demesne manors and boroughs; moreover, these creations had been effected with such apparent impunity as to suggest that, following the intrusion, no Welsh lord continued to rule in *Subboscus*, that it became a demesne manor belonging to Beaumont. *Subboscus* was certainly a demesne manor at the time of the earliest extant receiver of Gower's account (1366-7), for the account records that Welsh tenants were paying fixed rents (in lieu of renders) to the lord of Gower for their holdings, which they held in socage, meaning their tenure did not carry an obligation to do military service. Beaumont's successors, moreover, were apparently at liberty to give away parcels of land in *Subboscus* to religious institutions and to create new fiefs to such an extent that, by the early 14thcentury, *Subboscus* had shrunk to an area that now lies within the civil parishes of Gowerton and Llanrhidian Higher, and also that part of the ecclesiastical parish of Swansea that lay outside the Medieval borough; it was a territory that separated the Englishry of the Peninsula from the Welshry of *Uwch-coed*. This surviving part of *Subboscus* was 'full of woods, coal-veins, moors and wet ground' and was, therefore, of little use to the Anglo-Normans, reason for it to remain a Welsh-speaking enclave until the 19th century. The men of *Subboscus* had been allowed to live according to their time-honoured ways, for in 1348 Lord John Mowbray granted them a charter in which he confirmed 'all their laws and customs'. These laws—the Laws of Hywel Dda—were to remain in force until the Act of Union (1536) led to their replacement by English law, at which point what remained of *Subboscus* was absorbed into the Englishry.

Uwch-coed—known as *Supraboscus* in Latin text—comprised of the upland region that lies roughly to the north of the M4 Motorway. Beyond its southern foothills, *Supraboscus* was a place of high ridges separated by steep-sided valleys, even ravines. Throughout the Middle Ages it remained heavily forested according to both the records and the frequency with which *Ynys* is found in place-names such as Ynysforgan, meaning Morgan's Island; that is, an island clearing in a sea of woodland. Terrain such as this was ideally suited for Welsh guerrilla tactics, a debilitating death trap for Anglo-Norman troops. If a Welsh lord had held out against Beaumont's followers, *Supraboscus* is where he would have stood his ground.

Almost nothing is known of *Supraboscus* until the 1280s, but about three miles north of Clydach, at Grid Reference 694 047, on the western edge of a deep ravine, there is a 12th century earthwork called Cae-castell, believed to have been a Welsh attempt at constructing a castle, the reasons for the belief being that its construction is unusual and that, in the 12th century, no Anglo-Norman would have built a castle in such a remote and inaccessible place. The castle may have been the residence of a

Welsh lord who held his own against the Anglo-Norman intruders, or it may have belonged to one of several minor Welsh lords. Evidence in support of a minor Welsh lord who flourished in the late 12th century comes from several sources, the sum of which is that, during the late 12th century, one Cadifor ap Gwgan (a descendant of Maenarch, Lord of Brycheiniog) married Malt, daughter of Llywelyn Ychan, 'and thereby became possessed of the Lordship of Glyntawe [in western Brycheiniog] and part of Gower' as well. It may be that the marriage of Cadifor and Malt is bardic fiction, but in 1287, Gruffudd Frych, a later lord of Glyntawe, took part in a revolt against the then lord of Gower, William de Breos, and in order to obtain de Breos's peace he released his woods so that he might retain his other lands. Gruffudd's 'woods' later became known as the manor of Gwaun-Cae-Gurwen; the whereabouts of his 'other lands' in Gower are unknown.

By 1366-7 *Supraboscus* was a demesne manor, its people paying rent to the Anglo-Norman lords of Gower, their fixed rents collected (as in *Subboscus*) by a beadle. Prior to the Anglo-Norman intrusion a beadle would have been known as a *rhingyll*, who was responsible for collecting the renders due from free men, the perquisites of the lord's court, the heriots that were an early form of death duties and numerous other fines as well. In common with other parts of the Welshry, English law was introduced into *Supraboscus* as a result of the Act of Union.

Situated on the east bank of the Tawe, the land or lordship of *Cilfái* is somewhat of an oddity. It is not known whether it had been part of Gower in the Dark Ages, or whether it had been annexed as a result of Anglo-Norman intrusion or even the foundation of Neath Abbey. *Cilfái* was certainly part of Gower during the time of Henry de Newburgh (*c.*1138 - *post*-1166) as he is known to have granted fishing rights on the Tawe and at Pwllcynon to Neath Abbey. Following the surrender of Gower to Llywelyn the Great in 1217, Morgan Gam, Lord of Afan (1217-41), was enfeoffed in Landimore proper, Rhosili and *Cilfái* which he held of Llywelyn by the service of one knight's fee. Morgan Gam made Landimore proper and Rhosili the dowry of his daughter, Maud, on her marriage to Gilbert de Turberville, but Morgam Gam and his descendants frequently found themselves at odds with the Anglo-Norman lords of Gower over their title and continued possession of *Cilfái*, more so from about 1330 onwards. By 1366-7 *Cilfái* had become the personal property of the lords of Gower, which they administered as a separate lordship; henceforth, their possessions in Wales were referred to as the 'Lordship of Gower and Kylvey'.

The people of *Cilfái* were almost entirely Welsh and the free men, as a result of being tenants of the lords of Afan for over 100 years, were still paying the age-old food renders known as *gwestfa* in 1366-7 when Welshmen in other parts were paying their dues in the form of fixed rents. There was, however, a small Anglo-Norman/English community in the lordship, for Gerald, in his *Itinerary through Wales,* mentions that he stopped briefly at the Chapel of St. Thomas. By the 17th century it becomes clear that the hamlet of St. Thomas was part of the Swansea Parish.

A Welsh Manor

An exemplum of a Welsh manor, albeit on a much smaller scale, may be gleaned from the *Black Book of St. David's*, which records a survey carried out in 1326 of the bishop's manor of Llangyfelach (Clase). The survey records:

> as lord of the manor the bishop had a house there, with a plot of land worth 12d. yearly; a water mill in ordinary years worth four marks. The pleas and perquisites of the manorial court were worth 26s. 8d. yearly; the bishop and his tenants had [rights of] common in the lord of Gower's woods—worth £4. 1s.

The bishop's demesne amounted to 26 acres on which 'there ought to be sown ... oats, each acre worth to let 2d. yearly'. About half the demesne had reverted to the bishop, for there are references to plots ranging from a ¼ to 8 acres that had formerly been held by nine *taeogion* (although they are not described as such), all of whom were presumably dead at the time of the survey. It can, therefore, be assumed that the remaining acreage was held by the descendants of *taeogion* who were still living. A tax known as *commorth* was levied on the bishop's demesne at the rate of 1½d. per acre. The tax, which was due to the lord of Gower, was paid by the person or persons who held portions of the demesne at a given time, be it the bishop or the *taeogion*. The bishop 'also had in different parts 6¾ acres of meadow, each acre worth yearly to let 2d'.

Twelve men were empanelled as jurors for the purpose of the survey, all of them probably free Welshmen who resided in the manor. The last man to be listed as a juror, David Gogh ap Predith, was undoubtedly a free man; his name would certainly not have been placed at the end of the list if any of the other jurors had been *taeogion*. It is held that the jurors were the only free men to reside in the manor, but there are hints in the survey that they were not the only ones, the most obvious hint being a reference to the heirs of Iorwerth ap Payn. All the free men were, no doubt, members of any one of seven kindred groups called *gwelyau*, which appear to have been listed as follows: 'the first gwely Ieuan ap Kedivor; the second gwely Seyssill ap Gwyaun' and so on. As individuals the free men were liable to give the bishop 'for an heriot [their] best beast; if there were no beasts 5s.'. Collectively, they paid the bishop 10s. (originally a tribute in the form of food renders) on All Saints Day (1 November). They were also liable to render, collectively, on 1 May every third year, a *commorth* to the lord of Gower, consisting of four marks in lieu of eight beasts (cattle). There were services to be rendered to the bishop as well: each year they had to rebuild and thatch the bishop's mill-house, clean out the weirs as often as necessary and do suit at the mill, meaning they were obliged to grind their corn there. They also did suit at the manorial court, but difficult cases were dealt with at the bishop's palace at Lawhaden in Pembrokeshire. If anyone was taken into custody, they had to guard that person and escort him to Lawhaden at their own expense.

The total value of Llangyfelach was £5 16s. 7d., more than treble the value of the bishop's manor of Llandewi. When the finding of these surveys are compared one with the other they highlight the different personalities of Welsh and English manors; moreover, similar conditions to those at Llangyfelach must have existed within the manors of *Subboscus* and *Supraboscus*, as well as the lordship of *Cilfái*, although in the case of *Cilfái* there were periods when the tenants there were subject to the Welsh lords of Afan.

Anglo-Norman Administration

There can be no doubt that Beaumont's administrators made *Sweynsea* their head-quarters. The principal officer was the *seneschal* (steward), whose prime concerns were security within the lordship and the administration of justice by presiding in the lord's court and in the manorial courts that were held in the lord's demesne manors, including those in the Welshry. The earliest references to a *seneschal* relate to the period between 1184 and 1203 when Gower was Crown property. The references appear in royal documents known as Pipe Rolls, which were letters addressed to royal officers, instructing them on matters to do with administration. An entry in the Pipe Rolls for 1187 makes it plain the *seneschal* in that year was William de Londres, grandson of the William who, 'through fear, left the castle that was in his charge'— but William (the grandson) may have been *seneschal* before 1187, for he is the first witness to Earl William's charter of *c.*1170.

It was common practice for powerful men to appoint lesser Marcher lords to administer their possessions in Wales. It is, therefore, reasonable to assume that Beaumont would likewise have chosen an experienced man of the March such as Payn de Turberville or the William de Londres who was mentioned in 1116. Another important officer was the constable, the man responsible for the security of *Sweynsea* Castle. A charter of *c.*1200 establishes a William Revel as the earliest known constable at *Sweynsea*. The only other officer of note was the receiver, though whether this office existed in Beaumont's day is an open question. A receiver of Gower's account exists for the financial year beginning Michaelmas 1366. It is from this and later accounts that it is learnt that the receiver was responsible for compiling an account of the revenues and expenses relating to the lordship. As most of the lords of Gower were, like Beaumont, non-resident the receiver was also responsible for delivering the net profit to the lord's principal residence, or to locations desig-nated by royal officers whenever the lordship was in the custody of the Crown.

The Bounds of the Lordship of Gower

The earliest description of the bounds of the Lordship of Gower is among the miscel-laneous documents that are incorporated in the *Breviate of Domesday*. A translation of the Norman-French used to define the bounds in *c.*1300 reads:

> [The river] Loughor as far as [the river] Amman separates Gower from [the commote of] Carnwyllion; [the rivers] Amman and Llynfell as far as Clawdd Owain separates Gower from [the commotes of] Is-cennen and Perfedd; [the river] Twrch separates

Gower from the land of Brecknock; [the river] Tawe separates Gower from the land of the Earl of Gloucester [that is, the Lordship of Glamorgan] as far as its confluence with [the river] Glais; from Glais to the Meinihirion [a standing stone on Mynydd Drumau]; from the Meinihirion to the Crymlyn [a stream that ran through the Crymlyn Bog]; from Crymlyn to Pwllcynon [Cynon's Pool]; from Pwllcynon to [the river] Nedd; from Nedd to the sea.

In many respects the division of Gower into Welshry and Englishry resembles the division of Wales into *Pura Wallia* (independent Wales, usually the more mountainous areas), and *Marchia Wallia* (conquered Wales; that is, the March, usually the more fertile lowlands which invariably became Anglicized at an early date, except southern Pembrokeshire where, in 1108, according to the *Brut*:

a folk of strange origin and customs ... were sent by the King [of England] to Dyfed. And they occupied Cantref Rhos near the estuary of the River Cleddau and drove away the inhabitants. The folk [the Flemmings] came from Flanders ... because the sea had overwhelmed [their] land and thrown sand all over the ground, making the land unfruitful.

As to the jigsaw-like arrangement in Gower of fiefs, ecclesiastical manors and walled boroughs, this resembled the political fragmentation of Wales during the 200 or so years of intermittent warfare that ended with the death of Llywelyn the Last in 1282. During this period Welsh chroniclers found it expedient to refer to the petty kings of Wales as princes and/or lords, the reason being that Welsh rulers owed at least a nominal allegiance to the kings of England as, indeed, the leaders of Welsh society in Gower owed allegiance to Anglo-Norman lords such as Beaumont. Between *Pura Wallia* and *Marchia Wallia* lay a band of territory in which Anglo-Norman influ-

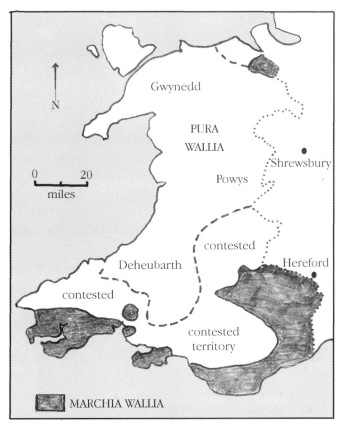

Wales in the 13th century.

ence was usually minimal and where control fluctuated between Welsh princes and the Anglo-Norman Marcher lords, or even the Crown.

Communications

Trackways that existed in the Dark Ages continued in use during the Anglo-Norman period when, for the first time, through routes appear in the records. The safest route to *Sweynsea* from Aberafan led to Neath, then probably ran in a south-westerly direction over Coed Ffranc (to the east of Crymlyn Bog), but Gerald, in his *Itinerary through Wales*, mentions the hazards he encountered on his approach to *Sweynsea* by a shorter route in 1188:

> As we approached the Nedd, which is the most dangerous and inaccessible river in South Wales, on account of the quicksand, which quickly engulfs anything placed upon it, one of the packhorses, the only one possessed by the writer of these lines, was almost sucked into the abyss. It was eventually pulled out with some difficulty, thanks to our servants, who risked their lives in doing so, though not without damage done to my books and baggage.

As the ford at Briton Ferry could not be located 'after heavy rain and floods', Gerald had to cross the river by boat. He, then, continued his journey over the Crymlyn Burrows till he came to the Tawe Estuary. He does not say how he crossed the Tawe, but a charter of 1306 mentions 'the Ferry of Sweyn'. This was by no means a safe passage as the ferry boat, which crossed the estuary near where Sainsbury's store stands today, ran the risk of being swamped by freshets. It was, no doubt, possible to cross the estuary on foot, for in 1898 one E.E. Rowse wrote:

> Heavily laden waggons ... would ford the river (near the present-day barrage) when the tide was out. Cattle and horses, even litters of pigs, crossed the river when the tide was at its lowest.

After leaving *Sweynsea*, Gerald passed 'through the plains in which Hywel ap Maredudd of Brycheiniog ... gained a signal victory over the English'. The 'plains' probably relate to Garn Goch Common, and it is likely that Gerald approached these wind-swept heights by way of *Hackedeweye* (mentioned in the charter of *c.*1170), which apparently followed the line of Pentregethin Road to Cadle Mill; from there, Gerald journeyed towards the treacherous waters of the Loughor Estuary.

Deer Parks

The Anglo-Norman lords of Gower took their hunting seriously, creating deer parks where game could be reserved for their own pleasurable pursuit. The earliest reference to a deer park in Gower is in Bishop Anselm's confirmatory charter of 1230, which mentions *Silva de Bruiz*, later known as Parc le Breos. The park consisted of some 2,000 acres of woodland, its bounds still traceable today by the remains of an earthen bank that originally carried a palisade, the ditch being on the inside. Within these bounds the woods and wild animals were protected by the laws of *vert* and *venison*. A hunting lodge existed at what is now Parc-le-breos House. The park was still in use in 1401-2 as the receiver's account for that year records a Richard More as parker there. The area was disparked later in the 15th century, some of it allocated to tenant farmers. An unenclosed deer park also existed in the heavily wooded Clyne Valley, and is referred to in a charter of 1306.

The Church under the Anglo-Normans

When the Anglo-Normans arrived in Wales they found a church that was somewhat alien to them, one that, although Catholic, needed to be brought in line with the Church of Rome. The Welsh clergy were opposed to change and had, therefore, to be dealt with; in a monastic church that meant focusing on the monasteries, stripping them of their wealth and influence. In dealing with the monastery at Llandaff the Anglo-Normans did away with the *claswyr* and eclipsed the subsidiary monasteries that still existed at Llancarfan, Llanilltud Fawr and elsewhere. They also seized, as we have seen, numerous properties belonging to Llandaff, including six in Gower. There were, however, two properties in Gower that belonged to the bishop of St. David's, neither of which appear to have been troubled by the Anglo-Normans. The former *clas* and later manor of Llangyfelach was unsuitable for manorial cultivation, which may explain why it was left in peace, but the tiny manor of Llandewi was a thoroughly Anglicized and fertile holding when it first came to light in 1326, at which point it becomes clear that the manors of Llangyfelach and Llandewi were, like Bishopston, separate lordships within the Lordship of Gower, the tenants of both subject to the jurisdiction of St. David's.

It would appear that the monasteries and cells that had existed in Dark Age Gower were all defunct by the time of the Anglo-Norman intrusion. Churches that had once served monastic communities appear to have become parish churches, for the Llandaff Charters record that Herewald, Bishop of Llandaff (1056—1104), had ordained a succession of priests at the former monasteries of Llangyfelach and Llangenydd. As to the statement in the Llandaff Charters which reads: 'in which church [Llangenydd] Bishop Herewald ordained Caradog, a holy and religious man, to be a monk', this has to be treated with caution, for Caradog lived a solitary life on the Island of Burry Holms before removing himself to Pembrokeshire shortly before the arrival of the Anglo-Normans.

There were at least 15 churches in Gower at the time of the Anglo-Norman intrusion. There may have been other ancient churches such as St. Illtuds, Oxwich, that do not appear in the records until after *c.*1150. There may also have been others that were rededicated to saints more acceptable to the Anglo-Normans. All Saints, Oystermouth, for example, may have originally been dedicated to St. Illtud. Apart from the 15 churches mentioned above, a further 25 or more foundations are known to have existed at some time or other during the period of Anglo-Norman domination; that is, in the 12th, 13th and 14th centuries. Of the 40 or so foundations that can be ascribed to this period, about half were Anglo-Norman dedications to St. Mary, St. John, St. Andrew and other non-Welsh saints; about three quarters of the total were sited in the Peninsula.

There is no evidence that the Anglo-Normans desecrated Welsh churches. What they did over a period of time was to grant some of them (and also a few dedicated to saints of their choosing) to religious institutions that were usually based outside Wales so that the 'land, tithes, oblations and sepultures' could be used to finance the said institutions. Mention has already been made of Beaumont's gift of four churches and land to a Norman abbey, and also Maurice de Londres' gift of Oystermouth church to an abbey in Gloucester. In 1156 Beaumont's widow, Margaret, granted the Church of Llanmadoc and the land appertaining to it to the military-religious Order of Knights Templar, so as to help finance its activities in protecting pilgrims in the Holy Land. In c.1165, William de Turberville granted 'the Church of Llanrhidian, with its Chapel of Walterston, the Church of Landimore (Cheriton) and the Church of Rhosili' to the military-religious Order of Knights Hospitaller, the tithes of these churches being used to finance treatment of sick pilgrims in the Holy Land. By 1231 this particular order was in possession of a total of nine Gower churches and a chapel. One of the most interesting endowments in later times was Bishop Henry de Gower's grant of property and the tithes of St. Mary's Church to the (hospice) Hospital of St. David in *Sweynsea*, where several chaplains ministered to 'priests, blind, decrepit or infirm and also other religious men'.

A 12th-century Church

The oldest surviving Medieval churches in Gower are of late 12th to 13th century date, being identified by their massive towers. It can only be assumed that the buildings that had previously occupied these sites were destroyed by Welsh insurgents. There are, however, the remains of a stone-built, 12th-century chapel on Burry Holms. Built over the wooden church that is mentioned in Chapter Three, the ruinous walls of a rectangular nave, measuring 5.33m. by 3.42m., show that the chapel was set in the usual east-to-west alignment with a doorway in the south wall. The eastern end of the nave originally had a semi-circular chancel, which was later replaced by a larger, square-shaped chancel. The chapel was very small, and although it served a community of monks, it nevertheless resembles the ruinous stone-built chapel of Llanelen, which served a secular Welsh community.

Although somewhat lager, the layout of a 12th century church was probably similar to the two chapels mentioned above, for a chapel during this period was usually a small church subordinate to a parish church. Llanelen was subordinate to the Church of Llanrhidian, whereas the chapel on Burry Holms was subordinate to a monastic foundation, that of Llangenydd Priory. Private chapels existed in the later stone castles at *Sweynsea*, Oystermouth and Weobley. Chapels associated with holy wells existed at Trinity Well, Ilston, and St. Peter's Well, Caswell, where excavation has revealed a stone-built well, a chapel and a priest's 'cell'.

Monks and Laity

The only physical evidence of a monastic community in Gower during the Anglo-Norman period are the remains of buildings that surround the stone-walled chapel on Burry Holms. Immediately south of the chapel there were several 12th-century dwellings and a 13th-century rectangular hall with rounded corners. Another building of 14th-century date occupied the sloping ground to the north, the tiered stone seating within pointing to its use as either a school of an assembly room. These building had obviously been built for the benefit of an ecclesiastical community of which the records are silent. The community had become defunct by the 15th century as several royal documents refer to the site as a hermitage.

College Farm, which now occupies the site of the mainland priory at Llangenydd, is of no archaeological value, but the records are consistent that the priory was usually occupied by a Benedictine prior and a companion monk, both of whom would have been French-speaking. The prior was responsible for managing the land mentioned in Beaumont's grant of c. 1119. The locals would have regarded the prior as an alien, the representative of foreign landowners, whereas the prior may been apprehensive about his Welsh neighbours. This state of affairs certainly existed elsewhere, as exemplified by a letter written by Gilbert Foliot, Abbot of Gloucester, to a Benedictine prior at either Ewenni or Cardigan who was apparently fearful of his Welsh neighbours.

> I recommend you strengthen the locks on your doors, [Foliot advised], and surround your house with a good ditch and an impregnable wall lest the people whom you say, gaze [at you] with shaggy brows and fierce eyes, break in and destroy with one blow all your labour and sweat. [Foliot, then, tried to reassure the prior by saying] We see, indeed, our own people take little account of the fear of God and reverence for His sanctuary, but we hear that the Welsh diligently honour holy places and persons consecrated to God.

Foliot' comments on the Welsh were reiterated by Gerald some 40 years later when he wrote, in his *Description of Wales*:

> The Welsh show greater respect than other nations to churches and ecclesiastics, to the relics of saints, bells, holy books and the Cross, which they devoutly revere; hence their churches enjoy more than ordinary tranquillity.

The church at Llangyfelach enjoyed 'tranquillity', for the bard, Gwynfardd Brycheiniog, described it, in the early 13th century, as a 'stately church ... where there is happiness and devotion'. Those who fostered 'respect' and 'tranquillity' were obviously the parish priests as monks were not responsible for the pastoral welfare of secular communities. What the situation was within the parish of Llangenydd is not known, although it is possible that the priors installed vicars to minister to the local Welsh. The Benedictines at Llangenydd certainly did not recruit Welshmen into their order (at least, not until the 15th century), nor did they earn the respect of Gerald who, despite being more Anglo-Norman than Welsh, criticized one of their priors for having an affair with a local girl, which led to the prior being deposed.

Neath Abbey

Llangenydd, with the land appertaining to it, was one of several ecclesiastical manors, the others being Bishopston, Llandewi, Llangyfelach/Clase, Llanmadoc and St. Johns near *Sweynsea*. The biggest ecclesiastical landowner was Neath Abbey, founded in 1130 with the arrival of French-speaking monks of the Order of Savigny, who took possession of the wasteland between Gower and the River Nedd. Seventeen years later, as a result of a merger on the Continent, the monks at Neath became white-robed Cistercians, whose austere way of life and sheep-rearing economy won the respect of the Welsh, drawing many of them into their order from Gower and from all over south-east Wales to the extent that, by the early 13th century, the abbot exercised authority over as many as 40 monks and two or three times as many lay brothers. Although they were renowned for their hospitality, the Cistercians were not above criticism, for whenever they were gifted land they had a tendency to evict some if not all the locals to make way for the creation of a grange, which was, then, worked by a small community of lay brothers. Neath Abbey created four granges in Gower—Cwrt y Carnau, Paviland, Cilibion and Walterston—all of which involved the removal of at least some tenant farmers.

Neath Abbey.

Effigies

There are no interments in Gower that can be definitely ascribed to the Anglo-Norman period, but there is an effigy and a tomb associated with members of the de la Mare family. The de la Mares first appear in a confirmatory charter of Bishop Leia (1176-97), which records the gift of Robert de la Mare to the Hospitallers, viz. the Church of Port Eynon and land in the fiefs of both Oxwich and Port Eynon. In *c.*1233 a Robert de Penres purchased the marriage of Agnes, daughter and heiress of William de la Mare, thereby possessing himself of her late father's fiefs. This suggests that the family had expired in the male line, but at the close of the 13th century members of a cadet branch appear in the records as the mesne lords of West Llangenydd, which they held by the service of a knight's fee. It was in memory of a member of this branch of the family that an effigy, known as *Dolly Mare*, was fashioned in *c.*1260. The damaged effigy in Llangenydd Church, is that of a knight in a style of chain-mail armour that became fashionable from the late 12th century onwards. The armour consists of a hood (coif), a long-sleeved tunic and leggings that were held in place by leather shorts. A surcoat conceals much of the knight's chain-mail, and the remains of shield— smaller than the kind used in Beaumont's day—is strapped to his

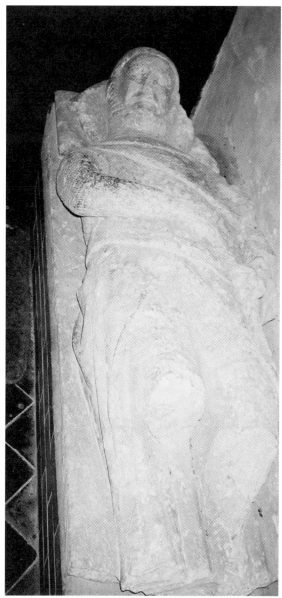

The effigy known as Dolly Mare *(de la Mare) in Llangenydd Church.*

back. The knight does not wear one of the flat-topped, round helmets with slits for forward vision that would have been fashionable in his day, but there is a leather band around his coif that would have helped to keep such a helmet in place. The position of his right arm athwart his chest, the hand gripping a sword, is said to be an indication that the man had been a crusader, but experts question this claim.

Doolamur's Hole—*a tomb in Oxwich Church.*

Whether the man had been a knight in the accepted sense is not known. The distinction between a 'knight' who held the non-hereditary title of 'sir' and an un-titled man-at-arms came into existence in the early 12th century. In Gower, men holding the title of 'sir' first appear in records relating to the 13th century, but only members of the de Breos and the de Penres families were knighted with any frequency.

The tomb known as *Doolamur's Hole* (de la Mare's Hole) is partially hidden in a recess in the north wall of Oxwich Church. The tomb carries two effigies, one of a knight in mixed plate and chain-mail armour, which dates the tomb to the 14th century, and the other of his wife in flowing robes. The position of the woman's effigy on the knight's right suggest that she had been an heiress, and that the knight had possessed himself of the fief of Oxwich as a result of his marriage to her. If the knight had been a member of the de la Mare family, then he must have belonged to the Llangenydd branch of the family.

The return of a de la Mare to Oxwich appears to have been short-lived, for members of the Penres family are known to have held the fief in 1320-23, 1352 and 1383. The de la Mares appear to have been sympathetic toward the Welsh in that the churches at Oxwich and Port Eynon retained their dedications to Welsh saints; moreover, the last member of the Llangenydd branch of the family, William de la Mare, lost his fief in the early 15th century for taking sides with the Welsh during the rebellion of Owain Glyn Dwr.

Two incised grave-slabs are also to be found in Oxwich Church, one having a Latin inscription that reads: 'Hugh, formerly the pious rector of St. Illtud's Church lies here' and is probably of 13th-century date. The other slab probably marked the grave of William de la Lake, rector of Oxwich 1320-23, who was involved in a dispute with the

A grave-slab with an inscription relating to a 13th-century rector of Oxwich Church.

then Lord of Oxwich, Sir Robert de Penres. Three more gravestones are at the western end of Llangenydd church. The inscribed stone fixed to the wall at eye level carries the unlikely distinction that it originally marked the resting place of St. Cenydd, whereas the grave-slabs at ground level were probably retrieved from the graves of two Benedictine priors.

Dioceses

It has been a commonly held belief that the Anglo-Normans were responsible for the creation of territorial dioceses in Wales and that, prior to their arrival, the Celtic Church had consisted of federations in which 'mother' churches exercised control over dispersed 'daughter' churches. There is, however, evidence to suggest that territorial dioceses already existed in South Wales during the time of Herewald, Bishop of Llandaff (1056—1104). It is believed that Herewald enlarged his diocese in line with the territorial expansion of Caradog ap Gruffudd, King of Gwynllwg, who, prior to his death in 1081, had ruled from the Tywi to the Wye. In Gower, Herewald even went so far as to usurp property that belonged to the bishop of St. Davids, for at Llangyfelach he ordained two priests, 'Aggar ... and after him Clydo'.

Herewald's dominion over an enlarged diocese appears at first hand to have been brief, for his successor, Urban, informed Pope Calixtus II in 1119 that 'during the reign of William Rufus [1087—1100] there had been a great invasion of the diocese by ... the bishops of Hereford and St. David's', meaning that Llandaff had lost Cantref Bychan, Cydweli, Carnwyllion and Gower in the west, and Ystradyw, Ewias and Ergyng in the east. Then, in 1129, Pope Honorius II issued a bull to Urban, confirming his claim to an enlarged diocese. He also sent bulls to 'the clergy and laity' of Gower and the other disputed territories, commanding them to 'humbly render obedience to' Urban. The Pope had undoubtedly been influenced by several witnesses who swore that the disputed territories had been 'contained within the bounds of the diocese of Llandaff; that is, between the Rivers Tywi and Wye', and that they, or their fathers, 'had seen Urban's predecessor, Bishop Herewald, holding for 40 years the said territory quietly and without interruption', which suggest that Herewald may have had dominion over an enlarged diocese at the time of (or shortly after) his consecration in 1056. Despite the bulls of 1129, the dispute over the seven territories continued until, in 1131, Pope Innocent II decreed that the issue should be remitted to London where three arch-bishops decided against Urban in 1133, with the result that Ergyng was returned to Hereford and the other six territories, including Gower, passed to St. David's. Llandaff was left with a diocese that coincided with the former kingdom of Morgannwg, plus one small manor in Gower—Bishopston—which remained a part of the diocese until 1920. Urban died in 1134 on his way to Rome to appeal against the decision and the matter was never raised again.

Conclusion

In retrospect the Anglo-Norman intrusion had a considerable impact on the lowland areas of Gower—but their domination, as we shall see, did not go unchallenged.

CHAPTER V
Conflict and Coexistence

The de Newburghs

Beaumont, his wife and their descendants held Gower for almost 80 years, and the family tree below shows their succession. Little is known of them personally, except that Beaumont is said to have had a 'studious and retiring disposition', whereas his eldest son, Roger, has been described as 'more addicted to pleasure than gifted with courage'. His grandson, William, is supposed to have been a 'handsome waster of his possessions', and is best known for his charter to the burgesses of *Sweynsea* (*c.*1170). Shortly before his death in 1184 William mortgaged Gower and this led to the lordship becoming Crown property. Nothing is known of the nature of Beaumont's other son, Henry, who appears to have been one of the few Anglo-Norman lords of Gower to reside in the lordship. Indeed, his stay in Gower proved so lengthy that in Earl William's returns of 1166 he is referred to as Henry de Gower.

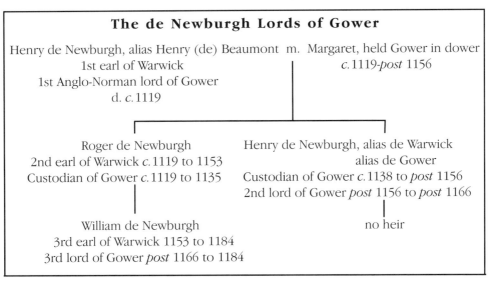

The de Newburgh Lords of Gower

Henry de Newburgh, alias Henry (de) Beaumont m. Margaret, held Gower in dower
1st earl of Warwick   *c.*1119-*post* 1156
1st Anglo-Norman lord of Gower
d. *c.*1119

Roger de Newburgh
2nd earl of Warwick *c.*1119 to 1153
Custodian of Gower *c.*1119 to 1135

Henry de Newburgh, alias de Warwick
alias de Gower
Custodian of Gower *c.*1138 to *post* 1156
2nd lord of Gower *post* 1156 to *post* 1166

William de Newburgh
3rd earl of Warwick 1153 to 1184
3rd lord of Gower *post* 1166 to 1184

no heir

Twelfth Century Incursions

The de Newburghs' hold on Gower did not go uncontested as the lordship frequently became a target for the belligerent princes of South Wales. The first recorded incursion into Gower occurred in 1116 when Gruffudd, the son of Rhys ap Tewdwr (d.1093), 'sent his companions to make an attack ... upon a castle ... at Abertawe ... And after burning the outer castle, and after the keepers had saved the tower and some of his men had been killed, he turned back'. It is not known whether Gruffudd's assault on a second unnamed castle had been part of this incursion, or whether it had taken place at a later date that same year. In either event the outcome of the first attack was that 'many young hotheads gravitated to Gruffudd from everywhere and carried off many spoils'. Gruffudd's attempt at re-establishing his father's kingdom failed a few months later when his followers were routed near Aberystwyth and he was forced to take refuge in the wilds of Ystrad Tywi.

In 1116 Gruffudd had neither the capability to defeat the Anglo-Normans in a straightforward fight on open ground, nor the expertise to take a strong castle outright; furthermore, he failed to rally the support of a generation that had learned to be circumspect. The men who dominated the succeeding generation differed in that they were not haunted by the devastating warfare of the 1090s; they were also men who had learned a thing or two from their Anglo-Norman neighbours. All they awaited was a favourable occasion, and when the storm broke on 1 January 1136 the prospect of Welsh independence took on a new lease of life, even in Gower, which is where the revolt started. According to a clerk in the service of a bishop of Winchester,

> on King Henry's death ... the Welsh, who always sighed for deadly revenge against their masters, threw off the yoke which had been imposed on them by treaties, and issuing in bands from all parts ... made hostile inroads in different quarters, laying waste the towns with robbery, fire and sword, destroying houses and butchering the population. The first object of their attack was ... Gower ... and hemming in with their levies on foot the knights and men-at-arms who, to the number of 516, were collected in one body, they put them all to the sword. After which, exulting in the success of their first undertaking, they overran all the borders of Wales.

Gerald provided further details when he wrote, some 50 years later, that after leaving *Sweynsea* he made his 'way hence towards the River Loughor through the plains in which Hywel ap Maredudd of Brycheiniog ... destroyed the English of those parts [presumably Gower and its environs], and many foot soldiers, in pitched battle'. The battle, which probably took place on Garn Goch Common, had been occasioned by the death of a strong king, though why Hywel ap Maredudd, who held sway over western Brycheiniog, should advance on Gower in inexplicable. The fact that he offered battle to more than 500 Anglo-Norman troops on open ground suggests that he did so in strength, having drawn support from many districts, including Gower. The aftermath of battle must have been horrific; according to Florence of Worcester the bodies of the fallen were 'horribly dragged about the fields and devoured by wolves'.

The outcome of the battle was that, locally, the Englishry was ravaged and, for the next three or four years, Gower was subject to a Welsh lord, Hywel ap Maredudd presumably. Elsewhere the revolt spread with disastrous consequences for the Anglo-Normans in West Wales. By the close of 1136 several princes, including Hywel ap Maredudd, had not only united to reduce a number of castles in northern Ceredigion, but they had united a second time under the princes of Gwynedd to fight another pitched battle near Cardigan, one in which the Anglo-Normans lost about 3,000 men. The battle in Gower had given the Welsh the confidence to go on the offensive—not only in 1136, but time and again over the next 150 years.

According to the missing Cartulary of Neath Abbey, Gower was reconquered by Henry de Newburgh—possibly in *c.*1138—although his hold on Gower was by no means firm, for in 1151 he appears to have been powerless to prevent another incursion from West Wales, one in which the sons of Gruffudd ap Rhys 'laid siege to the Castle of Aberllwchwr [Loughor] and burned it and ravaged the land'. Even when Gower was held by the Crown between 1184 and 1203 the incursions from West Wales continued. In 1189 the lordship was overrun by Rhys ap Gruffudd, and in 1192 Rhys 'besieged the town [of *Sweynsea*] for ten weeks, and the townspeople would have been forced to surrender through starvation, but for' the dissension that arose between Rhys's troublesome sons. The picture, however, is incomplete, for the history of Gower during the 12th century is fragmented. The *Brut*, for example, records the incursions of 1116, 1151 and 1189. Yet it does not mention the monumental battle of 1136, nor the ten-week siege of 1192—references to these events are to be found in different sources. It, therefore, follows that there were probably other incursions into Gower of which nothing is known; moreover, the records fail to give any indication as to how the Welsh of Gower responded to these incursions, or whether they were involved in uprisings of their own. The earliest reference to the belligerence of at least some Gower Welshmen does not appear in records until the late 13th century.

By the late 12th century the Welsh had become formidable opponents for two reasons, one being that, by the time of Gerald's itinerary through Wales in 1188, the men of South Wales, especially those of Gwent, excelled in the use of longbows, the arrows of which could penetrate chain-mail with ease. The other reason is that they had become adept at taking castles, though there is little indication as to how they carried out their assaults. The *Brut* records that the Welsh were using slings and catapults in 1193, but in 1198 'they were laying siege to [Painscastle] without any recourse to catapults and slings. And when the Saxons learned that, they were amazed'. Seventeen years later, when all the subsidiary castles in Gower were taken within a matter of days, the only reference to their destruction was that they were burnt, either during or after the assaults. It is tempting to speculate on whether their longbows—which must have provided effective support in an assault—may have been used to deliver fire arrows at the wooden walls of 12th century castles; they would have had a devastating effect on the inflammable buildings within a bailey.

Sweynsea Castle may have had too strong a garrison to be taken even with the aid of fire arrows—hence the ten-week siege in 1192. The threat of fire, however, could not be ignored, and when *Sweynsea* was threatened by Rhys Ieuanc's advance in 1215 'the garrison burnt the town'. This must have been a controlled burning to prevent the spread of fire while the garrison was primarily engaged in defence; it also denied the enemy the advantage of getting too close to the castle, using the cover afforded by town buildings. The ploy worked in that it deflected Rhys Ieuanc to carry out his attacks elsewhere. Despite the questionable claim that the castle was one of nine that were either taken or surrendered at the close of 1215, there is no direct evidence that *Sweynsea* Castle ever fell to a Welsh assault. The town of *Sweynsea* was, however, burnt by the Welsh on several occasions.

Thirteenth-Century Incursions

In 1203 King John granted Gower to his crony, William de Breos, only to take it back in 1208 when William upset him. Then, when King John upset his Welsh allies in 1212, the town of *Sweynsea* suffered for his lack of tact. Evidence for this comes from the *Annales de Margam* which records, somewhat tersely, that 'Rhys the Fierce [also known as Rhys Gryg] burnt Sweynsea'. Worse was to follow in that, for their loyalty to King John, the English of Gower suffered yet another incursion in 1215. The evidence is provided by the *Brut*, which records that Rhys Ieuanc (the Younger) advanced on Gower from the west

> and burned the Castle of Loughor. Thereupon he made for the Castle of Hugh de Meules at [Llandeilo] Talybont, and the garrison assayed to hold it against him, but he took it by force and burned some of the garrison and slew others. The following day he made for Seinhenydd [the Welsh word for *Sweynsea*], and for fear of him the garrison burned the town, but he, not desisting from his intention, made for the Castle of Oystermouth where he encamped that night. On the following day he burned both the castle and the town [meaning the village]. He [then] took all the castles of Gower before the end of three days and returned home joyfully victorious.

One of King John's rebel barons, Reginald de Breos, took possession of Gower at the close of 1215 and, to secure his rear, he placed himself and his extensive possessions on the Welsh border under the protection of Llywelyn ab Iorwerth, Prince of Gwynedd. Then, in 1217, Reginald changed sides, thereby incurring the wroth of Llywelyn, who marched on Brycheiniog and went on the rampage, after which, according to the *Brut*, Llywelyn

> led his host over the Black Mountains, where many of his packhorses were lost, and encamped at Llangwig. When Reginald ... saw the damage that Llywelyn had inflicted upon his territory, he took six knights with him and surrendered himself to Llywelyn, and on the following day he surrendered the Castle of *Sweynsea*, which Llywelyn entrusted to the keeping of Rhys Gryg. And there Llywelyn stayed for a few days before moving on to Dyfed.

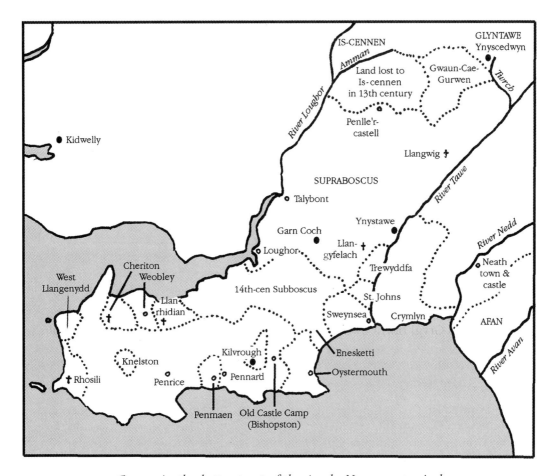

Gower in the latter part of the Anglo-Norman period.

Llywelyn took no territory for himself in his bold march through South Wales. What he wanted was the allegiance of the petty princes and leading men of the south; hence his reason for giving *Sweynsea* Castle and, indeed, most of Gower to Rhys Gryg, which he held as Llywelyn's vassal. At the time, Rhys Gryg was lord of greater part of Ystrad Tywi and Cydweli; with most of Gower in his possession he re-established the 11th-century territorial grouping of Ystrad Tywi, Cydweli and Gower.

Morgan Gam, Lord of Afan, also benefited from Llywelyn's policy of allegiance in that he became possessed of *Cilfái*, Landimore and Rhosili, which he held of Llywelyn by the service of one knight's fee. Another beneficiary may have been Gruffudd Gwyr (*fl.* late 12th to early 13th century) who is said to have held Ynyscedwyn, which lay just beyond Gower's north-eastern border, between the angle formed by the Rivers Twrch and Tawe. According to Rice Merrick, Gruffudd was a younger 'son of Cadifor' (Lord of Glyntawe), who 'came in company of ... who conquered that country [Gower] and had part thereof given him, who was therefore called Gruffudd Gwyr [Gruffudd of

Gower] ... of the sundry conquests thereof'. Parts of the text are missing, but the man who 'conquered that country' was Llywelyn and he must have passed near or through Ynyscedwyn on his way to Llangwig. It is, therefore, likely that Gruffudd Gwyr was one of many prominent men to join Llywelyn in his march on Gower; as a reward Gruffudd become possessed of the fief of Knelson.

The *Brut* records that, after Llywelyn had left Gower,

> Rhys Gryg destroyed the Castle of Sweynsea and all the castles of Gower ... and expelled all the English that were in the land without hope of their ever returning, taking as much as he pleased of their chattels and placing Welshmen to dwell in their lands.

What can be conjectured from this is that Rhys Gryg, who burnt *Sweynsea* in 1212, may have encountered opposition to his rule, which he countered by destroying the castles of Gower and expelling all the English. There is evidence that castles were destroyed, but historians have tended to play down the expulsion, despite the corroborative evidence of a bard who, extolling the exploits of Rhys Gryg, wrote:

> And Abertawe, town of calm
> Broken towers, and today is there not peace
> And St. Clears and the bright happy lands
> Not English, the people who possess them
> In Abertawe, strong key of England
> Are not the women altogether widows?

Both the *Brut* and the verse state that the English were expelled, not the Anglo-Normans, the reason being that, by 1217, the Anglo-Normans had come to regard themselves as Englishmen, despite the fact that many of them still spoke French. This development towards national awareness had been transmitted to Welsh chroniclers who, from the late 12th century onwards, no longer distinguished between French and Saxons, but had reverted to using one word to describe the intruders from the east—*Saesneg*, meaning English.

As to the expulsion, the evidence as it stands suggests there had been trouble at *Sweynsea* in which blood was spilled. Elsewhere, Rhys Gryg 'expelled all the English that were in the land', which may well be an exaggeration as the customary tenants were no threat to him. The people most likely to oppose him were the principal men within the Englishry, in particular the mesne lords who were also prominent burgesses; it was, after all, their castles that he destroyed. Evidence in support of this assumption is slight, but in 1241 Henry III issued instructions for Philip Hareng— whose father (or grandfather) had been *disseised* in the war between King John and Llywelyn—to be restored to the fief of Penmaen which, in the intervening years, appears to have been held by one John Blancagnel. In addition the *Brut* says that Rhys Gryg, after expelling the English, placed 'Welshmen to dwell in their lands', and both Morgan Gam and Gruffudd Gwyr became mesne lords, presumably at someone else's expense. The local *uchelwyr* would also have used the occasion to further their own interests.

Rhys Gryg's hold on Gower proved short-lived. In 1218 Llywelyn made his peace with King John's son and heir, Henry III, but his attempts at persuading Rhys Gryg to surrender Gower to Reginald de Breos came to nought until, in 1220, he invaded Rhys's territory and forced him to hand over the lordship, not to Reginald as the Crown would have wished, but to Reginald's nephew, John de Breos. Thus began an era in which Gower was ruled by a family whose members became renowned for their duplicity, extortion, tyranny, wasteful extravagance and unpaid debts. The de Breoses were, to some extent, resident lords, although their main residence was in the Honour of Bramber in Sussex, to which Gower became inextricably linked from 1226 onwards.

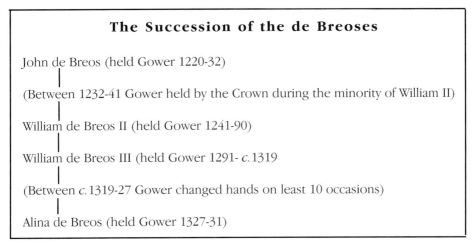

The Succession of the de Breoses

John de Breos (held Gower 1220-32)

(Between 1232-41 Gower held by the Crown during the minority of William II)

William de Breos II (held Gower 1241-90)

William de Breos III (held Gower 1291- *c.*1319

(Between *c.*1319-27 Gower changed hands on least 10 occasions)

Alina de Breos (held Gower 1327-31)

Sweynsea's First Stone Castle

What John de Breos is remembered for most is that, in 1221, he 'repaired the Castle of *Sweynsea* by the leave and council of Llywelyn' who was his overlord at that time. Past historians have referred to this entry in the *Brut* as the occasion—or start date—when *Sweynsea* Castle was rebuilt in stone; this would more or less coincide with the ten-year period when Carmarthen Castle was also rebuilt in more durable material than wood, but it has to be said that *Sweynsea* Castle could have been rebuilt in stone during the 20-year period following the siege of 1192.

The location of the ditch that is associated with what later became known as the 'outer bailey' has already been outlined in Chapter Four. Suffice to say that the 1975 excavation beneath David Evans' store showed the ditch here to have been more than 3m. deep, its width at the top just over 10m., the sides sloping at 45 degrees to a flat bottom almost 3m. wide. Small sections of the wall have been uncovered on the north, west and south, apparently sited on the slopes of the knoll, except on the east where it overlooked the steep slope to the Strand. Several documents refer to towers that were positioned at various points on the wall—Donelstour, Singleton's and

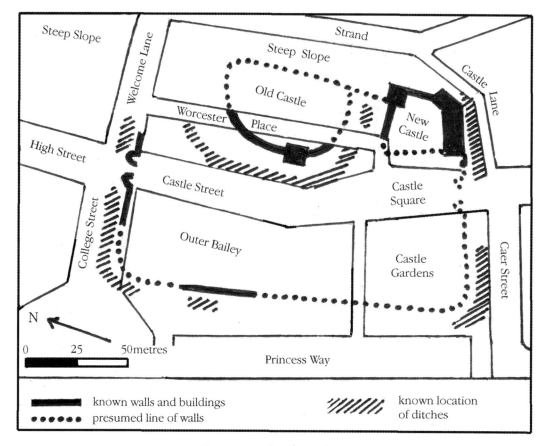

Sweynsea *Castle* c.1300.

Bokynham—but their exact locations are unknown. The earliest reference to this stone-walled 'outer bailey' dates to the time of William de Breos II (1241-90). According to an inquisition of 1319, William II had sold 'to Walter de Pecar, what was formerly the [north] gate of the outer bailey ... with two towers adjacent thereto, and also, to William ab Ithel, the south gate of the same bailey'.

Part of the stone wall and ditch of what later became known as the 'Old [inner] Castle' (not the ruins of *c.*1300 that can be seen today) was revealed in the 1913 excavation between Castle Street and Worcester Place. When Colonel Morgan wrote of what had been uncovered he described the remains of a curtain wall, in places up to 2m. high, that formed the western face of a D-shaped 'inner castle'. At the southern end of the curtain wall a platform, 9m. square, projected beyond the wall and is believed to have been the base of a strong keep. Both the curtain wall and the platform were fronted by, firstly, a slope and then a ditch at least 2m. deep. The rebuilding of both the 'inner' and 'outer castle' in stone would undoubtedly have led to an economy in manpower, and the 13th-century garrison at *Sweynsea* may have been similar to the one recorded at Carmarthen in 1228—30 men-at-arms and 10 crossbowmen.

Other Defence Works

It is difficult to determine what happened to the majority of subsidiary castles that were destroyed by Rhys Gryg. The evidence, such as it is, suggests that some them were never reoccupied; this would appear to have been the case at Castle Tower, Penmaen, and Old Castle Camp, Bishopston, where excavations have unearthed pottery of 12th and early 13th century date, but no later. Conversely, the huge keep at Oystermouth Castle and also the hall at Pennard Castle are believed to be of mid-13th century date, confirming that these two sites were reoccupied, though there is no evidence to suggest that their outer defences were anything other than paling. Loughor Castle, on the other hand, already had a stone gate-tower prior to its destruction in 1217 (on the site of the ruined tower that can be seen today); this was presumably repaired and a curtain wall raised around the perimeter of the former ring-work. It is not known exactly when this work was carried out, but it bears a resemblance to the stone-built defences of *Sweynsea's* 'inner castle'. Another castle, built on a hitherto undefended site to guard against incursions from Is-cennen, was that of Penlle'r-castell. It has been said that this castle was never finished, but it may have been

The impressive tower of Llanrhidian Church.

destroyed in 1252 during a border war between William de Breos II and Rhys Fychan (a grandson of Rhys Gryg), Lord of Dynefwr and the eastern half of Ystrad Tywi. In 1306 a jury stated that Rhys Fychan had burnt a castle of the said William called the new castle of Gower.

The four castles mentioned above may all have been belonged to the de Breoses, which may explain why they were built/rebuilt in stone, partially or otherwise. Stone keeps were also built by mesne lords at Penrice and Weobley, both of them on hitherto undefended sites and both dated to the mid-13th century. One reason for the mesne lords' apparent reluctance to rebuild extensively in stone is that, within the Englishry and the three ecclesiastical lordships of Bishopston, Llangyfelach and Llandewi, there was a development towards converting churches into strongholds where the local population could take refuge and defend themselves against Welsh insurgents. This development may

Cheriton Church, built to provide defence in the late 13th-early 14th century.

have begun in the late 12th century, but most of the old churches in the Peninsula—those with strong towers—were probably built in the early 13th century.

The walls of both the chancel and nave of any church designed to withstand attack are noticeably thick, originally having narrow windows high up in the walls, the roofs flagged for obvious reasons. Two massive oak doors, reinforced with bands of iron, barred entry into the nave, but should the attackers gain access their next objective would be the tower that was usually attached to the western end of the nave. The tower at Llanrhidian is impressive, the more so when allowance is made for the fact that the outside door and large windows are later insertions. On the first floor there is a blocked-up doorway that would have led into a room above the nave, one that enabled crossbowmen to shoot at attackers in relative safety. The final place of retreat was at the top of the tower where hourding made it possible for crossbowmen to cover all sides of the church except the east side of the chancel. In effect the hourding created a large, overhanging, wooden box, or room, around the battlements. There are at present 12 tower churches in Gower, the latest being Cheriton, purpose-built in the late 13th or early 14th century. To these may be added the tower at Llangyfelach, which stands alone as the church to which it had been attached no longer exists. A 17th century sketch shows that St. Marys, *Sweynsea*, also had a strong tower.

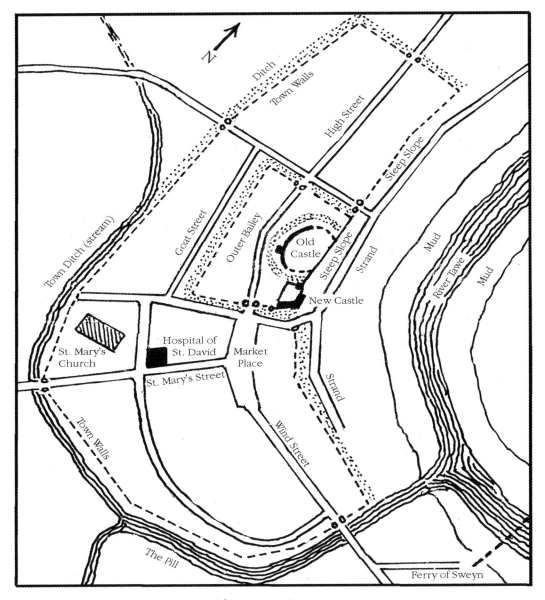

14th-century Sweynsea.

Sweynsea's Town Defences

Siege mentality is also evident at *Sweynsea* where nature itself provided features that could be utilized for defence. On the east, from the castle northwards to High Street Station, a scarp dominated the River Tawe, an ideal location for either paling or a stone wall. Two streams—the Pill and the Town Ditch—provided natural obstacles on the south and west. Only on the north did the town lack natural defences, but the deficiency would have been made good by an artificial ditch as far back as the early 12th century. Ditches required periodic clearances; sometimes they needed to be recut. Any remains of a town ditch can, therefore, only be relevant to a late stage in its existence. A section of ditch, similar to the one associated with the outer bailey, has been uncovered to the west of St. Mary's churchyard wall. Another section in the shape of a wide-angled 'V' has been found in the vicinity of King's Street. The different shapes of the two sections suggest that they were cut or recut at different periods.

In the 12th century the town ditch must have been backed by a bank and paling which, in later times, were replaced by a stone wall bonded with lime mortar. Small sections of walling have been uncovered at several locations, mostly in the vicinity of St. Mary's Church where crenellation has been found in the ditch. No date can be assigned to any section of walling, nor can it be said that the wall had been built as a single undertaking. The earliest reference to a section of town wall appears in the foundation charter of the Hospital of St. David, dated 1332, which refers to land 'next to the wall of Sweynes'. This date may be relevant as the burgesses obtained two 'murage and paving' grants—one in 1317 for a period of ten years, and one in 1338 for a period of five years—which gave them the right to levy tolls on a variety of goods that came into the town, the money raised being used to build or repair the town walls. Murage is also mentioned in a charter of 1306, and it is reasonable to assume that there were earlier grants of this nature of which we know nothing.

Llywelyn ap Gruffudd

In 1256 Llywelyn ap Gruffudd, Prince of Gwynedd and grandson of Llywelyn ab Iorwerth, went on the offensive and, in doing so, soon made himself master of the greater part of Wales. Then, in the spring of 1257, a large force of English troops left Carmarthen, intending to restore order in the Tywi Valley and dislodge Llywelyn's vassal, Maredudd ap Rhys Gryg. The force was ambushed and routed with a loss of over 3,000 men; few made it back to Carmarthen. This appalling disaster brought Llywelyn south to conduct a successful campaign in West Wales. According to the *Annales Cambriae*, Llywelyn then turned eastwards:

> to the land of Cydweli, Carnwyllion and Gower, where he burnt all that belonged to the English in the aforesaid land, as also in Abertawe, and having subjugated all the Welshmen thereof he joyfully returned home at Easter.

The following year Llywelyn assumed the title of 'Prince of Wales', but in 1277 his plans to make Wales a strong feudal state suffered a setback when he clashed with the recently crowned Edward I. Overwhelmed by the forces that were ranged against him, he was forced to submit to humiliating terms. Then, after six years of maladministration by Edward's officials, the petty princes of Wales rose in a carefully-planned rebellion on Palm Sunday 1282. Llywelyn joined the revolt only to be killed in a skirmish near Builth. His brother, David, fought on until he was captured and executed the following year. Welsh independence was, to all intents and purposes, at an end, although a few minor princes who had been loyal to the Crown continued to hold their lands as Marcher lords. There now remained only one place where the descendants of the *Britanni* still held out against the odds—Brittany, and there the Bretons were to retain their independence for a further 250 years.

The Attack of 1287

Wales may have been conquered, but its people were far from finished, for in 1287, according to the *Breviate of Domesday,* 'Disagreement arose between the king's seneschal of Carmarthen and Rhys ap Maredudd [ap Rhys Gryg] Lord of Dryslwyn', Cantref Mawr and two commotes in Ceredigion. Rhys rose in revolt on 8 June. He, then, fell

> upon Gower with a great army, [and] the Welshmen dwelling in Supraboscus joined with him; because of the advice of those men, in particular ... Einion ap Hywel ... [on 11 June he] suddenly and unexpectedly burned the town of Sweynsea, [and] attacked and killed the unfortunate people thereof ... [and took] away much spoil. A few days after this [he] swept down on the noble manor of Oystermouth, [taking] the castle [on 27 June], which ... William de Breos ... had built for himself; and certain men who were captured [Rhys] caused to be strangled before his eyes, others he led away captive. [Rhys also] violated the church for the sake of loot and slew the wives and children of the men ... .indifferently.

Rhys was soon forced to withdraw, unable to match the English forces that were advancing on Gower. Orders were issued on 2 July, directing that any Welshman who had taken part in the revolt should be received into the king's peace, the intention being to encourage defection. Among those to defect were Gruffudd Frych, Lord of Glyntawe, who offered his woods in *Supraboscus* so as to retain his other lands; also Gruffudd ap Hywel, Owain Fychan, Einion ap Hywel and others in *Supraboscus*, who requested that their lands should be subject to the English process of law—'the law of twelve and of inquest'—meaning that they and their tenants would be tried by jury as opposed to an assembly of landowners. Their request was by no means unusual as the men of Gwynedd had the choice of opting for a verdict by jury some 50 years earlier.

The above entries in the *Breviate of Domesday* are noteworthy for their detail and for providing the earliest reference to the involvement of Gower Welshmen in an incursion from West Wales. The 1280s are, moreover, a period when the history of Gower becomes increasingly more abundant. We know, for example, that William II was regarded by his tenants as a tyrant and an extortionist. In 1282 some of his English tenants migrated to Carreg Cennen (then in the hands of the Crown), declaring they would prefer to live under the King's officers. Two years later the Welsh in the north-western corner of *Supraboscus*—between the Cathan and the Amman Rivers—declared their lands to be part of Is-cennen. They were supported in their claim by the King's officers in Is-cennen. Despite an inquiry into the occurrence, the land between the Cathan and the Amman was never again a part of Gower.

In 1319 an *inquisition* was held concerning alienations that were believed to have taken place in Gower. The lordship was held of the king by the service of one knight's fee; therefore, Gower belonged to the king and no demesne within its bounds could be alienated; that is, sold off without the king's licence. The jury appointed to hold the *inquisition* found that William had illegally alienated numerous parcels of land, including the demesne manor of Trewyddfa, to both his English and Welsh tenants. It is likely that many of these alienations took place during the 1280s when William's desire for money was at an all-time high. One of the most interesting alienations is the one 'to William ab Ithel, the south gate of the [outer] bailey'—it is the earliest recorded instance in which a Welshman had been allowed to purchase property in *Sweynsea*. William II, of course, was half Welsh through his mother, Margaret, and this may have influenced his decision to appoint as his *seneschal* a man of Welsh origin, John Iweyn (Owain). Iweyn took up the appointment before 1274 and held it intermittantly for more than 30 years, during which time he proved himself to be as unscrupulous as his master and his master's son and heir.

William de Breos III

William de Breos II died in December 1290, but by 1288 his eldest son, William III, appears to have taken responsibility for Gower. William III had all the infamous qualities of his forefathers; he was also a capable soldier. Late in 1287 William raised a force from Gower, consisting of 7 horse and 63 foot, and from elsewhere a further 3 heavy horse, 18 light horse, 2 mounted and 19 foot crossbowmen and 400 foot. His orders were to take Newcastle Emlyn from the supporters of Rhys ap Maredudd; on 1 January 1288 he began blockading the rebel stronghold. Three weeks later, with the aid of a seige engine, he took the castle without losing a man.

William III succeeded to Bramber and Gower in March 1291. His 29-year tenure of Gower is important in that, during this period, there is a wealth of information both of the man himself and of the internal affairs of his lordship, all of which provides insight into what the people of Gower had to endure under a Marcher lord. From the start William proved to be a profligate, one who had no intention of honouring the huge debts that he had inherited from his father. In 1292 he was warned by King Edward I that if he did not settle his debt to the Crown, then royal officials would collect the money by distraint—but William temporized.

From 1294 onwards several opportunities arose that enabled William to evade his responsibilities by placing himself at the King's disposal, for whilst he was in the King's service he could not be sued. In September 1294 he set out to serve in an expedition to Gascony, only to turn back because of widespread revolt in Wales, the result of heavy taxation. William joined forces with three other noblemen to provide 50 lances for service in West Wales. After the revolt collapsed in the spring of 1295, he remained in service as 'keeper of the peace' until Easter the following year. Then he was away, serving in Scotland, not alone it seems, for when the campaign came to a close a safe-conduct was issued to 'twenty Welshmen of William de Breos, all of whom had served the King well in Scotland and were returning home'.

In 1297 he raised 200 infantry from Gower for service in Flanders; in 1298 he led 300 infantry from Gower into Scotland where they fought at the Battle of Falkirk. William's infantry were probably all Welshmen, most of them longbowmen, serving for pay. Evidence in support of this assumption can be gleaned from an entry in the *Patent Rolls* for 1362, which commands the Sheriff of Gloucester to 'survey all the archers whom the King had commanded to be arrayed in Gower, to remove such as were inefficient and send others arrayed in their place'. That same year a mandate was sent to the then Lord of Gower, Thomas de Beauchamp, to array 40 of his best Welsh archers from Gower and send them to Liverpool at the King's wages.

William must have had mounted men in his train—prominent *uchelwyr* to take charge of his Welsh foot soldiers; also the sons of prominent English landowners to serve as retainers as well as a few mesne lords from both Bramber and Gower. There is no evidence as to whether he had to provide infantry for the Scottish campaign of 1300, but when the feudal host mustered at Carlisle on 14 June that year, William de Breos was one of the many names to appear in the *Roll of the King's Host*, which also records that he offered the services of 3½ knights' fees for Bramber and one knight's fee for Gower, the man named in the last instance being Greffith de Goer, obviously a man of substance, possibly a mesne lord.

Evidence of William's wasteful extravagance in Gower is difficult to discern, but as a military man, possibly one with illusions of grandeur, he may have been respon-

Sweynsea's *New Castle, viewed from the south. The roadway to the left is the site of the south gate of the outer bailey.*

Oystermouth Castle, several times destroyed by the Welsh.

Pennard Castle, built c.1300.

sible for work on several castles, which his father may have commenced, but which he carried to completion in the late 13th or early 14th century. He was at least partly responsible for what became known as the 'New Castle' (the ruins of which can be seen today) at *Sweynsea,* built in the south-eastern corner of the outer bailey, adjacent to the Old Castle, which was subsequently allowed to decay. The restoration of

Oystermouth; that is, the erection of the southern *enceinte* (including the two round towers that were removed probably in the time of Cromwell) may also be attributed to him, as well as the curtain wall and gateway at Pennard Castle and the now ruinous gate-tower at Loughor. His involvement in defence works is supported by the fact that there were at least two periods during his rule when murage was levied for building or repairing the town walls at *Sweynsea*.

William's lust for money is evident in the *inquisition* of 1319, which shows that he had made four times as many alienations as his father, ranging from parcels of land to whole manors such as the former fief of Loughor, which he sold to his *seneschal*, John Iweyn, in 1302. Other alienations involved mills, coal mines near the Clyne, the ferry at *Sweynsea* and two towers of the 'outer bailey'. The earliest evidence of William's tyranny relates to 1299 when the Bishop of Llandaff complained to the King that William had trespassed in his manors of Bishopston and Murton, forcing his tenants there to attend the English County Court at *Sweynsea*, thereby depriving the Bishop of revenue. Prior to 1299, William had already been making excessive demands on his own tenants, for in a charter of 1306 there are numerous hints as to how he fleeced his *Sweynsea* burgesses, as well as references to forced loans. Even the mesne lords had their grievances as they were obliged—and no doubt considered it their privilege—to do suit at William's County Court where they served as jurors, upholding the customary 'law of 12 and of inquest'; by arbitration they settled the disputes that were brought before William's court. William, on the other hand, had no qualms about flouting the mesne lords' position in his court, especially as there was money to be made from issuing writs and from amercements (punishment by fines), the more so if he, or his *seneschal*, were calling the shots; moreover, as a Marcher lord, William claimed royal jurisdiction, thereby denying his tenants the right to appeal against his decisions in a higher court.

By the close of 1299 William's tenants had had enough and, without his knowledge, took their grievances to the King's County Court at Carmarthen. In the six years that followed, William held his own against his tenants and the royal officers who were determined to strip him of his regal powers. On four occasions—in 1300, 1301, 1302 and in March 1305—he was summoned to Parliament to answer for his and his *seneschal's* misconduct, including that of imprisoning the mesne lord of Kilvrough, William de Langton, at Oystermouth in order to coerce him into dropping all charges that were pending. William's misgovernance was the subject of two major inquiries, the findings of which were annulled because William had been in Scotland at the time of the inquiries. Indeed, it was due to his involvement in the King's Scottish wars between 1302 and 1305, coupled with the fact that the King wished 'to deal gently with' him, that William managed to frustrate his opponents for so long.

William lost the King's favour in 1305 when his stepmother, Mary de Roos, finally had him in court over an outstanding debt of 800 marks. The judge had no sooner pronounced judgement in Mary's favour than William leapt over the bar and 'spoke coarse and contemptuous words' to the judge, with the result that William ended up in the Tower at the King's pleasure. The King became even more displeased when, in the Parliament of September 1305, he heard that William, despite several prohibitions, had aggrieved his tenants yet again by installing a sheriff in Gower, contrary to 'the law and customs of those parts'. The King commissioned three judges to hear and terminate the grievances of William's tenants 'unless the said William, before their coming to ... Sweynsea, shall ... do full justice to the ... tenants'. The court opened on 21 February 1306. A jury from West Wales soon nullified William's claims to royal jurisdiction, whereas the judges made it plain that, unless he came to terms with his tenants, he would be stripped of his regal powers.

The judges then proceeded to deal with the tenant's grievances, but none of the complainants appeared in court because William had already made an out-of-court settlement with them. Three days later William issued two charters of liberties—one to the 'burgesses of Sweynsea', and one to the 'abbots, priors, Hospitallers, Templars, knights, free tenants and their tenants and men, English and Welsh, within the English County of Gower'. He even guaranteed that, if he or his successors ever violated the liberties in either charter, they would pay a staggering fine of 500 marks to the king and 500 marks to the tenants. The charter to the men of the English County is primarily concerned with defining the 'law and customs of those parts', providing ample evidence as to how William and his officers had corrupted the judicature for the purpose of enriching themselves, even to the extent of selling and denying justice as they saw fit. The *Sweynsea* charter is concerned with redefining the privileges in Earl William's charter of *c*.1170, which William had contravened (opposite).

No charter was granted to the men of the Welshry, presumably because they had no grievances, William being reluctant to oppress them as they formed the bulk of his infantry, which he recruited for service in the King's host. It may be significant that, in 1303, prior to a campaign in Scotland, he appointed as his attorneys two men—Thomas de Quyntyn, presumably of Bramber, and Griffynum ap Mewryk of Gower, possibly the Greffith de Gower who did knight's service in 1300. To some extent William may have favoured his Welsh tenants. They were, however, discriminated against by their English neighbours as both charters state that no one 'shall be indicted ... by Welshmen ... or by any persons who are of the lord's household', to which the County charter adds, 'but only by twelve lawful and free men, not suspect'.

William—the Cause of Civil War

During the closing years of his tenure of Gower, William, through his greed, caused a great deal of distress throughout the realm. The trouble began when, in 1318, he made arrangements for his son-in-law, John de Mowbray, to succeed to Gower with the proviso that, in the event of his daughter, Alina, and her husband (Mowbray) dying childless, the lordship would pass to Humphrey de Bohun, Earl of Hereford. Despite these arrangements, William took steps to sell Gower to two other Marcher lords. He, then, proceeded to do business with King Edward II's favourite, Hugh Despenser, Lord of Glamorgan. While negotiations were in progress, Despenser got wind of

In preparing his defence William employed the services of the monks at either Neath or Margam Abbey. Memoranda in support of his claim to royal jurisdiction—some of it in Norman-French—was entered upon the fly-leaves of the Breviate of Domesday, the most notable entries being a copy of Earl William's charter of *c.*1170 to the burgesses of Sweynsea, a copy of King John's charter of 1203 (which records his grant of Gower to William's great, great grandfather, William I), a description of the bounds of the lord-ship and also material relevant to the history of Gower. William maintained that he and his ancestors had always enjoyed royal jurisdiction, basing his claim of King John's charter, which royal officials argued was nothing more than a land grant. William even tried to prove that royal jurisdiction had been enjoyed by the earls of Warwick in the 12th century; hence the mate-rial that is relevant to them.

In the *inquisition* of February 1306 a jury gave evidence to the effect that William's father had usurped royal jurisdiction during the Welsh war of 1257, that William's father had been aided and abetted in this by his father-in-law, Nicholas de Moeles, who was seneschal of Carmarthen at that time. William (the son) must have been aware of the weakness of his claims and, after the fall of Stirling Castle in 1304, he persuaded the King to provide him with a re-grant of King John's charter, one that included all manner of juris-diction and all royal liberties, which William used as a pretext to install a sheriff in the English County of Gower, but which the King's judges declared to be contrary to the law and customs of those parts. William must have valued his royal liberties as granted in the 1304 charter because, to keep them, he had to come to terms with his tenants in 1306 by issuing two char-ters that were meant to curb both his financial exactions and his oppression.

William's illegal alienations, and persuaded the King to institute an inquiry to ascertain the facts. Three judges met at Crymlyn in the summer of 1319 to compile a list of who had purchased what. The question, then, is who informed Despenser of what William had been up to?

John Iweyn had ceased to be William's *seneschal* before 1304, but the two men appear to have remained on good terms to the extent that Iweyn made several illegal purchases between 1311 and 1315 to become a landowner of considerable standing. By 1319 Iweyn was in the employ of Hugh Despenser and William may have presumed, perhaps rightly, that Iweyn had informed Despenser of the alien-ations. This assumption would explain why, on 4 August that year, the King ordered an investigation into:

the accusation of John Iweyn claiming that William de Breos (and others) had taken and carried away his goods at Gower and that they had conspired together at Sweynsea and Oystermouth ... to accuse the complainant of the death of Ifan ap Madoc ... and had procured his arrest and detention in the prison ... at Sweynsea; the King commanded the said William de Breos, if all these things were so, to do full justice to the said John Iweyn, but the said William has failed to do so.

Iweyn's misfortune may have been the result of a trumped-up charge; he was subsequently released and restored to his possessions. Despenser, meanwhile, had cause to be confident, for in a letter to his sheriff, dated 21 September 1319, he expressed his belief that Gower would soon be his. Unfortunately, sometime between the date of the letter and October the following year, John de Mowbray seized Gower on the strength of his contract with William. Despenser complained to the King. When a royal officer and his escort tried to enter the lordship in October, they had to turn back at St. Thomas because 'a great multitude of Welshmen' barred their way. A month later a larger force met no resistance, but the whole business of a Marcher lordship being taken into the King's hands on behalf of someone as despised as Despenser only served to antagonize many barons. Mowbray, the Earl of Hereford and several other barons invaded Glamorgan in May 1321, taking castles with relative ease, including Neath where they captured John Iweyn. *Sweynsea* Castle appears to have surrendered without a fight, its custodian sent to Brecon as a prisoner. Iweyn was less fortunate, being taken to *Sweynsea* where he was decapitated by a local baker.

When the fighting spread to England the King had no recourse other than to come to terms with the rebel barons. In August he pardoned Mowbray, allowing him to retain Gower. Within three months civil war broke out again, only this time the King gained the upper hand, routing the rebel barons in Yorkshire on 16 March 1322. Mowbray was captured and executed, his wife, Alina, and his young son incarcerated in the Tower. What part William played in these events is unknown, except that immediately after the cessation of hostilities he wrote to the King, excusing his absence from Parliament on the grounds of ill health. Two years later, when Alina described her father as 'frantic and not in good memory', Despenser made him institute a lawsuit for the recovery of 'the two commotes of Uwch-coed and Is-coed which constituted the whole of Gower'. With the King and Despenser on his side the result was a foregone conclusion, but within weeks William—who, by then, was probably a broken man—granted Gower to Despenser's father. William died in April 1326, his remaining estate passing to the Despensers.

Peace, but not coexistence

A serious Welsh uprising—the Revolt of Llywelyn Bren—took place in Glamorgan in 1316, but there is no evidence that the men of Gower were involved; nor is there any evidence of open hostility between the English and Welsh communities within the lordship throughout the 14th century. This does not mean that the two communities had entered a period of harmonious coexistence. On the contrary, there is likely to have been an element of mistrust between the two ethnic groups, as evidenced by the *Sweynsea* charter of 1306, which states that no burgess could be indicted by Welshmen for offences committed within the borough.

Both the survey of the manor of Llangyfelach (1326) and the alienations recorded in 1319 suggest that the Welsh within the Welshry were little effected by

Anglo-Norman/English influences with regards to kinship and land tenure. On a more positive note, both sources make it plain that the Welsh were using English currency in their transactions, and that some of them had been given what were then English names, William being a favourite in honour, perhaps, of their Lord William de Breos III, or his father. The cultural divide would, therefore, appear to have remained intact, but the borders between Englishry and Welshry were becoming somewhat blurred.

Initially the English had been largely confined to *Sweynsea* and the 'south side' of the Peninsula, but by the time of William de Breos III they were making inroads into areas that had formerly been occupied almost exclusively by the Welsh. The evidence comes from the *Penrice and Margam Abbey mss.*, which contain charters (dated between 1314 and 1320) connected with the sale, leasing and granting of land in the manors of Llangenydd, Landimore proper and Llanrhidian. The charters also show that some Welshmen in these manors were converting their holdings to English tenure. Equally revealing are the names of witnesses to the transactions, some of whom were mesne lords, which makes it possible to compile a list of those who held fiefs in Gower at that time. Other men involved in, or who were also witnesses to the transactions, were from a landowning class below that of the mesne lords, of which the records have hitherto been silent—the Anglo-Norman and English freeholders, men who owned their land, were permitted to serve as jurors in a court of law and who, in later times, were referred to as yeoman farmers.

Purchases by English freeholders and by *Sweynsea* burgesses in the same three manors and in *Subboscus* are also recorded in the list of alienations compiled in 1319, showing that expansion into Welsh areas was, in these circumstances, a direct result of William's greed. The alienation 'to Gillete and Agnes, his wife, 15 acres of land and four acres of meadow in Subboscus at Oystermouth and Enesketti [Sketty]' is noteworthy for several reasons, one being that Gillete had purchased land in what was then part of the Welshry. *Enesketti* lay between the demesne manors of Oystermouth and *Sweynsea*. At that time, *Enesketti* was part of the Welsh manor of *Subboscus*, but Gillete's purchase extended into 'Subboscus at Oystermouth', which suggest that a small Welshry existed within the manor of Oystermouth as well; this must have been in the less-fertile, northern half of the manor. How Welsh 'Subboscus at Oystermouth' and *Enesketti* were can be judged by the alienation 'to Roger ap Maeb and his brethren, 40 acres of land in Enesketti', which shows that land was still held by *gwelyau* even in this area. The evidence of both the *Penrice and Margam Abbey mss.,* and the alienations recorded in 1319 would suggest that men felt free to purchase land outside their cultural enclaves, but what these sources fail to show is that the two communities were still at variances.

Nowhere was the lack of coexistence more evident than in *Sweynsea* where, prior to 1400, only two Welshmen are known to have owned property in the town. The first was the William ab Ithel who bought the south gate of the 'outer bailey' from William de Breos II. The purchase did not make him a burgess, but he may have become a *chenser*, being permitted to practise a trade, but excluded from the privileges of the borough. John Iweyn, on the other hand, bought a tower from William de Breos III that had formerly belonged to Thomas de Singleton. He also purchased a messuage (a dwelling house with outbuildings and land) and in 1311 he received a grant from William III, stating that his purchases in 'the bailey of the castle' were to be held 'as an entire burgage'. Iweyn undoubtedly obtained the privileges of the borough through his association with William and not from the burgesses who would have been ill at ease about having Welshmen in the town.

Evidence of underlying tension between the ethnic communities in Gower comes not from official records, but from the fact that Welsh culture in the 14th century was very much alive. Itinerant bards still frequented the whitewashed halls of the *uchelwyr*, often voicing contempt for their English neighbours. One such bard, Gruffudd ap Maredudd, better known by his bardic name, Casnodyn, was a native of *Cilfái* who sang all over Wales between *c.*1320-40, praising the *uchelwyr* who did not speak the English tongue. Casnodyn and others like him were dependent on generous patrons such as Hopcyn ap Tomas of Ynystawe, near Morriston. Hopcyn was renown in his day as a cultured man, a collector of ancient manuscripts. He had at least five odes addressed to him, praising him as a brave warrior (presumably in the service of the Crown) a man of wisdom, an authority on bardic prophecy. He may even have been partly responsible for commissioning the *Red Book of Hergest*. Such was his fame that, in 1403, he was summoned to Carmarthen by the rebel, Owain Glyn Dwr, to prophesy on what might 'befall him'.

The Rule of John de Mowbray

John de Mowbray II was already in possession of extensive estates in the Midlands and in the North of England when, in 1331, he succeeded his mother, Alina de Breos, to Bramber and Gower. John was the first of a long line of non-resident lords whose visits to Gower were infrequent. Nevertheless, John's rule is noteworthy for several reasons, one being that in 1348 he confirmed to his tenants in *Subboscus* all their ancient customs and laws, thereby confirming that the two communities were still living according to their respective laws. What is also worthy of mention is that, in the early years of John's rule, two notable events took place in Gower, which illustrate the cross-border warfare that must have been going on intermittently for centuries. In 1334 men from Is-cennen plundered Gower, though not without suffering loss. The following year the men of Gower returned the visit, killing nine Is-cennen men and capturing others whom they imprisoned at *Sweynsea* Castle. Mowbray was not involved in either occurrence, but he was, nevertheless, a distinguished soldier, loyal to the King. He was several times called upon to raise troops from Gower for service in France—in 1341, 123 men; in 1343, 150 men; in 1346, 100 men 'all armed with a pennoned lance or a good bow'; in 1351, 30 men for service in Yorkshire.

Changes brought about by Wars and Plagues

The endless wars with France finally led to an Act of Parliament that was to extinguish the linguistic identify of the Anglo-Normans. In 1362, by the Statute of Pleading, Norman-French ceased to be the language of the lawcourts and, for the first time, English was spoken in Parliament. Norman-French may have continued in use among the aristocracy for a generation or more, but on this the records relating to Gower are silent. Nor are the records much help in providing evidence that the 14th century witnessed the growth of a more accepting relationship between the English and Welsh communities other than, between 1384 and 1394, a Welshman, Robert ap Thomas, was *seneschal*. Only in *Sweynsea* is there a suggestion of coexistence between the two communities, for in 1400, when the lordship was in the hands of the Crown, the King issued instructions for a third of Gower and a third of *Sweynsea* to be assigned to Elizabeth, Duchess of Norfolk, as her dower. The assignments in *Sweynsea* were mostly burgages, or part burgages, and were recorded in the dower deed, street by street, along with the names of the 63 burgesses who owned them. Many of the burgesses owned more than one burgage. John Fairwood, for example, owned 5½ burgages and may have owned other burgages in the two-thirds of *Sweynsea* that remained in the hands of the King. What is significant is that ten burgesses—possibly 13—had names that show they were Welsh, or of Welsh origin.

That some Welshmen were accepted as burgesses may, in part, be attributed to the Black Death that devastated Wales in 1349-50, to return with diminishing severity in 1361-2, 1369 and on several other occasions in the late 14th century. There is no record of the Black Death in Gower, but a seafaring town such as *Sweynsea* would not have escaped visitations by the plague, which would have spread with diminishing severity into the lowland areas, leaving the uplands only lightly affected; this in turn may have occasioned the movement of Welshmen into English dominated areas, including *Sweynsea*. The Black Death was also instrumental in eroding the distinction between the free and unfree in both Welsh and English communities. Depopulation through death or flight led to a severe shortage in the labour services of the unfree, so much so that landowners had no recourse but to lease their depopulated demesne to both free and unfree men on terms more favourable to the tenants, thereby creating a tenure known as copyhold.

The Last Revolt

The best indicator to the relationship between English and Welsh communities is in records relating to the first decade of the 15th century when segregation, inequality, financial exactions, administrative incompetence and the dislocation brought about by plagues all conspired to initiate a carefully planned and co-ordinated revolt in North Wales, which began in September 1400 when Owain Glyn Dwr declared himself 'Prince of Wales'. Although Gower was far removed from the trouble, the authorities at *Sweynsea* were sufficiently alarmed to repair both the castle and the 'outer

Weobley Castle, destroyed by the Welsh between 1403-5.

bailey', the walls of which were 'broken and thrown to the ground'. The rebellion spread southwards and on 6 July 1403 Owain took Carmarthen by surprise. At the time it was stated in a letter that Owain felt 'quite sure all the castles and towns in Cydweli, Gower and Glamorgan [would be taken] for the [men of those] same countries have undertaken the sieges of them till they are won'. Weobley Castle was certainly destroyed by Welshmen, the evidence coming from an *inquisition post mortem* of 1410. Another *inquisition post mortem* the same year revealed that the two-thirds of Gower in the King's hands was valued at only £100 per annum 'because the lordship and land for the greater part had been devastated by Welsh rebels'.

Within a month of taking Carmarthen, Owain had carried the war into Glamorgan and must, therefore, have passed through Gower. *Sweynsea* was evidently still holding out at the time because, in September, several ship owners were commissioned to deliver supplies 'for the soldiers and others dwelling in the castle and town of *Sweyneseye*'. Nothing more is known of the situation in Gower until the summer of 1405 when, on 26 June, the King confirmed the charter of 1306 to the men of the English County. The following year the rebellious Welshmen of Gower made their submission to the King. There is, however, a tradition that the English of Gower supported the rebellion; while it is true that named Englishmen throughout Wales are known to have defected to the rebels' cause, only one such person appears in the records relating to Gower—William de la Mare, and he had his fief of West Llangenydd confiscated.

The Anglo-Norman Legacy

Palaeolithic hunters and Mesolithic hunter-gatherers left only artefacts to testify to the millennia they spent roaming the Gower plateau. In all that time little or no impact was made on the landscape until Neolithic farmers arrived to clear woodland and leave megalithic monuments to hint at their settled way of life. Cairns and barrows show that Bronze Age men occupied both the uplands and the plateau that, by then, had become a peninsula. Iron Age men left their mark by constructing hill-forts; they may even have given Gower its Celtic heritage. The Roman army departed after occupying the land for 60-70 years, leaving little to show of its military skills, but after 300 years of Roman rule the free *Britanni* had come to see themselves as privileged men, the descendants of Roman citizens. What they left behind as the *Cymry* was their language and a heritage that speaks of their determination to be free and to retain their cultural identity.

By contrast the Anglo-Normans lost their language and their cultural identity, but left an indelible mark on the landscape, for they were the people who shaped Gower, being responsible for establishing two boroughs, several castles, more than a dozen fortified churches and, above all, stamping an English identity on the coastal landscape; they also promoted trade. Both the designation of lordship and the division into Englishry and Welshry were to continue until the Act of Union of 1536 abolished the Laws of Hywel Dda so that law and justice could be 'administered in Wales in like form as it is' in England. The terms Englishry and Welshry were, therefore, no longer relevant, but today the City and County of Swansea bears a similarity in its extent to the old English County of Gower.

The arrangement whereby mesne lords could demand service dues from the servile peasantry within their fiefs gradually gave way, from the late 14th century onwards, to manors in which landowners were supported by a rent-paying tenancy and a few casual labourers. The manors in turn have all gone, but in many instances their bounds have survived as parish boundaries, whereas tower churches and the castle ruins at Weobley, Loughor, Oystermouth, Penrice, Pennard and *Sweynsea* still serve as a reminder of Gower's Anglo-Norman past.

The borough of Loughor did not grow until the coming of the industrial revolution; even then its growth was limited. *Sweynsea,* on the other hand, expanded beyond its walls in the Medieval period, its population becoming increasingly Welsh. In 1835, when the population within the old borough stood at over 13,000, *Sweynsea* became a municipal borough and was, therefore, freed from the control of both the lord and his *seneschal*. Being ideally situated for seaborne trade it is hardly surprising that it has become Wales's second city.

Language versus Identity

The most abiding accomplishment of the Anglo-Normans was to establish an English colony on the 'south side' of the Peninsula. From the 14th century onwards the descendants of these early colonists gradually imposed their language and their way of life on the indigenous Welsh in the Peninsula while they, themselves, took on a Welsh identity.

Further Reading

1. *The Royal Commission on Ancient and Historical Monuments in Wales, Glamorgan*, Volume One: *Pre-Norman*, Part One, *The Stone and Bronze Ages*, Part Two, *The Iron Age and Roman Occupation*.

2. *Geraldus Cambrensis: The Itinerary through Wales and the Description of Wales*, translated by Sir Richard Colt Hoare.

3. *Pre-historic Gower* by J.G. Rutter.

4. *The Liber Landavensis* (The Book of Llandaff) by W.J. Rees.

5. *The History of Swansea and of the Lordship of Gower*, Volume One (1920) by W.H. Jones.

6. *Morganiae Archaiographia* by Rice Merrick – Ed. By Brian Ll. James.

7. *History of West Gower*, Four Volumes by Revd. J.D. Davies (1877-94).

8. *Welsh Tribal Law and Custom in the Middle Ages*, Two Volumes by T.P. Ellis.

9. *Brut y Tywysogion* (The Chronicle of the Princes), *Peniarth ms. 20 Version* (1952) and the *Red Book of Hergest Version* (1955) both by Thomas Jones.

10. *A Source Book of Welsh History* by Mary Salmon.

11. *The Castle of Swansea* by Colonel W. Ll. Morgan (1924).

12. *Edward Lluyd and his Correspondents in Glamorgan: a view of Gower in the 1690's.* Translation by the Honourable Society of Cymmrodian.

13. For a modern translation of some of Swansea's early charters see *Medieval Swansea Factsheet 1—Swansea Charters* by Bernard Morris.

14. For a modern translation of the *Breviate of Domesday* and the *Missing Cartulary of Neath Abbey* see 'The Swansea and Glamorgan Calendar', an unpublished ms. by W.C. Rogers (1943-45).

15. *Swansea, its Port, Trade and their Development* by E. Harris contains a translation of Florence of Worcester's description of the battle that took place between Swansea and Loughor.

16. *The Welsh Wars of Edward I* by J.E. Morris contains several accounts of the men of Gower's involvement in the campaigns against Llywelyn, Prince of Gwynedd.

17. *A History of Gower* by Derek Draisey provides a chronological history of Gower from Roman times to the mid-19th century (first edition 2002—revised second edition 2003).

Index